DISCOVERING AMERICA

The Northwest

ALASKA • IDAHO • OREGON • WASHINGTON

By
Thomas G. Aylesworth
Virginia L. Aylesworth

WITHDRAWN

CHELSEA HOUSE PUBLISHERS
New York • Philadelphia

First Printing

1   3   5   7   9   8   6   4   2

Library of Congress Cataloging-in-Publication Data

Aylesworth, Thomas G.
    The Northwest: Alaska, Idaho, Oregon, Washington
Thomas G. Aylesworth, Virginia L. Aylesworth.
    p. cm.—(Discovering America)
    Includes bibliographical references and index.
    Summary: Examines the geography, history, culture, and people of
Washington, Oregon, Idaho, and Alaska.
    ISBN 0-7910-3406-2.
        0-7910-3424-0 (pbk.)
    1. Northwest, Pacific—Juvenile literature. 2. Washington (State)—Juvenile literature. 3.
Oregon—Juvenile literature. 4. Alaska—Juvenile literature. 5. Idaho—Juvenile literature. [1.
Washington (State). 2. Oregon. 3. Idaho. 4. Alaska. 5. Northwest, Pacific.] I. Aylesworth, Virginia
L. II. Title. III. Series: Aylesworth, Thomas G. Discovering America.

F852.3.A95   1996   94-45824
979.5—dc20   CIP
                                           AC

CONTENTS

ALASKA   5

Alaska at a Glance   6
Places to Visit   13
Events   15
The Land and the   18
    Climate
The History   21
Education   26
The People   27

IDAHO   29

Idaho at a Glance   30
Places to Visit   36
Events   36
The Land and the   38
    Climate
The History   42
Education   47
The People   47

OREGON 49

Oregon at a Glance 50
Places to Visit 57
Events 58
The Land and the 62
Climate
The History 65
Education 68
The People 69

WASHINGTON 71

Washington at a Glance 72
Places to Visit 79
Events 80
The Land and the 84
Climate
The History 88
Education 90
The People 91

Further Reading 94
Index 95

Alaska

The state seal of the territory of Alaska was adopted in 1913. On the present seal, adopted in 1959, "state" was substituted for "territory." Pictured in the center are icebergs; railroads; forests; ships; native people; and symbols for mining, agriculture, fisheries, and fur seal rookeries. The northern lights shine above them, with "The Seal of the State of Alaska" printed in a circle surrounding the seal.

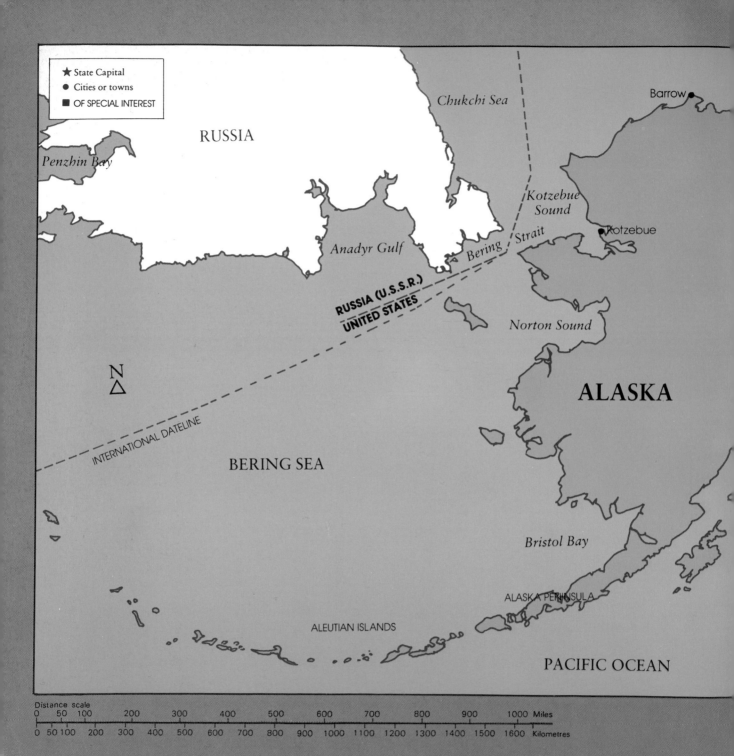

★ State Capital
● Cities or towns
■ OF SPECIAL INTEREST

RUSSIA

Penzhin Bay

Chukchi Sea

Barrow ●

Kotzebue Sound

Anadyr Gulf

Bering Strait

● Kotzebue

RUSSIA (U.S.S.R.)
UNITED STATES

Norton Sound

N
△

INTERNATIONAL DATELINE

ALASKA

BERING SEA

Bristol Bay

ALASKA PENINSULA

ALEUTIAN ISLANDS

PACIFIC OCEAN

Distance scale
0 50 100   200   300   400   500   600   700   800   900   1000 Miles
0 50 100   200   300   400   500   600   700   800   900 1000 1100 1200 1300 1400 1500 1600 Kilometres

ALASKA
At a Glance

ARCTIC OCEAN

Amundsen Gulf

NORTHWEST TERRITORIES

UNITED STATES

CANADA

● Fairbanks

—MOUNT MCKINLEY

YUKON

Anchorage
● Spenard

BRITISH COLUMBIA

MENDENHALL GLACIER■
★ Juneau

Gulf of Alaska

Sitka ●

Ketchikan ●

Capital: Juneau

State Flag

State Flower: Forget-Me-Not

State Bird: Willow Ptarmigan

Major Industries: Oil, gas, commercial fishing, tourism

Size: 591,000 square miles (largest)
Population: 586,872 (48th largest)

7

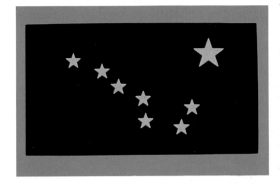

State Flag

In 1926, a contest to design a territorial flag was held among Alaska's schoolchildren. The winning design, submitted by 13-year-old Benny Benson, was adopted in 1927. The blue field stands for the Alaskan sky and fields of forget-me-nots; the seven gold stars forming the Big Dipper represent Alaska's gold mines; and the eighth star—the North Star—symbolizes Alaska's northernmost location. It was designated state flag in 1959.

State Motto

North to the Future

This phrase was adopted as the official state motto in 1967. It was chosen from among 761 entries in a competition won by Juneau newsman Richard Peter.

When George Vancouver was exploring the Alaskan coast in 1794, Glacier Bay was still occupied by a glacier.

State Capital

Juneau has been the capital of Alaska since it became a territory of the United States in 1912.

State Name and Nicknames

The name Alaska is taken from the word *alakshak*, used by the people of the Aleutian Islands to mean "mainland." After the United States bought Alaska from Russia in 1867, the name was applied to the territory and then to the state.

Although Alaska has no official nickname, it is often referred to as *Seward's Folly* or *Seward's Ice Box* because it was purchased for the United States by Secretary of State William Seward. Other nicknames include *Land of the Midnight Sun* and *The Last Frontier*.

State Flower

The forget-me-not, *Myosotis alpestris*, was adopted state flower and floral emblem by the legislature in 1949.

State Tree

In 1962, the Sitka spruce, *Picea sitchensis*, was adopted state tree.

State Bird

The willow ptarmigan, *Lagopus lagopus alascensis Swarth*, was chosen state bird in 1955.

State Fish

In 1963, the King salmon, *Oncorhynchus tshawytscha*, was named state fish.

State Gem

Jade was selected state gem in 1968.

State Marine Mammal

In 1983, the bowhead whale, also known as the right whale, was chosen state marine mammal.

State Mineral

The state legislature designated gold as the state mineral in 1968.

State Sport

Dog mushing, once an important means of transportation, was named the official state sport in 1972.

State Song

"Alaska's Flag," with words by Marie Drake and music by Elinor Dusenbury, was adopted as state song in 1955.

Population

The population of Alaska in 1992 was 586,872, making it the 48th most populous state. There are .84 people per square mile.

Industries

The principal industries of Alaska are oil, gas, tourism,

The governor's mansion in Juneau.

and commercial fishing. The chief manufactured products are fish products, lumber and pulp, and furs.

Agriculture

The chief crops of the state are barley, hay, greenhouse nursery products, potatoes, lettuce, and milk. Alaska is also a livestock state. There are estimated to be 7,500 cattle, 2,500 sheep, 37,000 reindeer, and 5,000 chickens and turkeys on its farms. Spruce, yellow cedar, and hemlock are harvested. Sand and gravel, crushed and broken stone, and gold are important mineral resources. Commercial fishing earned $1.6 billion in 1992.

Government

The governor and lieutenant governor, the only elected officials of Alaska, serve four-year terms. Other top executives, including the attorney general and the adjutant general, are appointed by the governor with the approval of the state

Logging is an important industry in Alaska.

legislature. The legislature, which meets annually, consists of a 20-member senate and a 40-member house of representatives. Alaska has 14 senatorial districts, six of which elect two senators each, and eight of which elect one each. Of the 27 representative districts, 13 elect two representatives each, and 14 elect one each. Senators serve four-year terms and representatives

serve two-year terms. The most recent constitution was adopted in 1956, three years before Alaska became a state. In addition to its two United States senators, Alaska has one representative in the U.S. House of Representatives. The state has three votes in the electoral college.

Sports

Sporting events on the collegiate and secondary

Alaska's Russian heritage is apparent in this Ninilchik church.

and it is the home of two military bases built after World War II: Fort Richardson and the present Air Force base, Elmendorf Field. More than half of the state's residents live in Anchorage.

> *Things to see in Anchorage:* Alaska Aviation Heritage Museum, Alaska Public Lands Information Center, Alaska Zoo, Alyeska Resort, Anchorage Museum of History and Art, Chugach State Park, Fort Richardson Fish and Wildlife Center, Heritage Library and Museum, Imaginarium, and Oscar Anderson House (1915).

school levels are played throughout the state. In addition, hunting, fishing, skiing, and dogsledding are popular pastimes. The most famous dogsled race, the 1,049-mile Iditarod Trail Race, is held annually in early March.

Major Cities

Anchorage (population 226,338). This modern city, Alaska's largest, sits on a high bluff overlooking Cook Inlet. Originally established as the construction headquarters for the Alaska railroad in 1914, it has become the transportation and business center of south-central Alaska. A year-round seaport, Anchorage is equipped to handle the oil shipments that are vital to its economy. Tourism in Anchorage has been growing significantly in the past years

Fairbanks (population 30,843). Established as a trading post in 1901 by Captain E.T. Barnette, Fairbanks lies near the geographical center of the state. When gold was discovered the following year, the settlement was flooded with prospectors, who named the town after Senator Fairbanks of Indiana. A second growth spurt occurred during World War II, when Fairbanks became the center of northern military defense. This boom continued in 1958 with the construction of a $250 million missile site at Clear, located 80 miles from Fairbanks. The latest significant growth spurt occurred in 1968, when oil was found in Prudhoe Bay, 390 miles to the north.

Things to see in Fairbanks: Cripple Creek Resort, Gold Dredge Number 8, National Oceanic Atmospheric Administration Satellite Tracking Station, Riverboat Discovery, University of Alaska Museum, Alaskaland, and Mining Valley.

Juneau (population 26,751). This capital city, occupying 3,108 square miles, is the largest American city in area. Leading industries include fishing, lumbering, mining, and tourism. In 1880, Joe Juneau, Richard Harris, and three Tlingit Indians found gold in this area and started the Alaska gold rush. In the next year over 100 miners

Autumn arrives in Anchorage, Alaska.

settled in this region and in 1900 Juneau was incorporated and made the new capital of Alaska. The gold mines were successful for more than 50 years, until they were finally closed in 1944.

Things to see in Juneau: Alaska State Museum and the Annual Golden North Salmon Derby.

Places to Visit

The National Park Service maintains 15 areas in the state of Alaska: Klondike Gold Rush National Historical Park, Sitka National Historical Park, Kenai Fjords National Park, Kobuk Valley National Park, Denali National Park and Preserve, Gates of the Arctic National Park and Preserve, Glacier Bay National Park and Preserve, Katmai National Park and Preserve, Lake Clark National Park and Preserve, Wrangell-St. Elias National Park and Preserve,

Noatak National Preserve, Yukon-Charley Rivers National Preserve, Cape Krusenstern National Monument, Admiralty Island National Monument, and Misty Fiords National Monument. In addition, there are 56 state recreation areas.

Haines: Fort William H. Seward. The first permanent army post in Alaska features a replica of a tribal house, a trapper's cabin, and totem poles.

Homer: Pratt Museum. This museum features Eskimo and Indian artifacts, a botanical garden, and a marine gallery.

Juneau: Alaska State Museum. Exhibits in this museum relate to native art and state history.

Kenai: Fort Kenay Historical Museum. This museum is housed in a replica of the log barracks that were part of a U.S. military post.

Ketchikan: Saxman Native Village. One of the highlights of this Tlingit Indian village is a totem park in which master carvers can be seen at work.

Kodiak: Kodiak National Wildlife Refuge. The refuge, occupying nearly 2 million acres of land, is set aside to preserve the natural habitat of the Kodiak bear, as well as other native animals.

Nome: Carrie McLain Memorial Museum. This museum contains exhibits that depict the city's gold rush years, in addition to displays on Eskimo art and archaeological artifacts.

Palmer: Musk Ox Farm. Guided tours are available on this farm, which is one of the few in the world where musk ox are raised

Petersburg: Clausen Memorial Museum. One of the displays features a world-record, 126½-pound king salmon.

Seward: Resurrection Bay Historical Society Museum. This museum is devoted to displays and artifacts of Alaska's—and Seward's—history.

Sitka: St. Michael's Cathedral. The cathedral contains an extensive collection of Russian orthodox art.

Skagway: Trail of '98 Museum. The museum contains elaborate displays on the cultures of the natives of Alaska.

The Tlingit leave their mark with this tribal house front at Ketchikan, Alaska.

Soldotna: Kenai National Wildlife Refuge. This refuge, which was established by President Roosevelt in 1941, has its headquarters in Soldotna.

Valdez: Valdez Museum. This museum has displays on the pioneer heritage of the city, in addition to exhibits on the Alaska Pipeline.

Wrangell: Wrangell Museum. The museum features displays of Tlingit Indian artifacts among its many exhibits.

Events

There are many events and organizations that schedule activities of various kinds in the state of Alaska. Here are some of them.

Sports: Iditarod Trail Race (Anchorage), Great Alaska Shootout (Anchorage), North American Sled Dog Championships (Fairbanks), Solstice Game (Fairbanks), World Eskimo Indian Olympics (Fairbanks), Yukon Quest International Dog Sled Race (Fairbanks), Alcan 200 Snowmachine Rally (Haines), Golden North Salmon Derby (Juneau), Salmon Derby (Ketchikan), Bering Sea Ice Classic Golf Tournament (Nome), Seward Silver Salmon Derby (Seward), All Alaska Logging Championships (Sitka), Sitka Salmon Derby (Sitka), Tok Race of Champions (Tok), Halibut Derby (Valdez), Pink Salmon Derby (Valdez), Silver Salmon Derby (Valdez).

Arts and Crafts: The Crafts Fair at UAA (Anchorage), Festival of Native Arts (Fairbanks), Athapaskan Old-Time Fiddling Festival (Fairbanks), Summer Arts Festival (Fairbanks), Alaska Folk Festival (Juneau).

Music: Anchorage Opera (Anchorage), Quiana Alaska Native Dance Festival (Anchorage), Basically Bach Festival (Anchorage), Chilkat Indian Dances (Haines), Sitka Summer Music Festival (Sitka).

Entertainment: Fur Rendezvous (Anchorage), Iceworm Festival (Cordova), Fairbanks Ice Festival (Fairbanks), Golden Days (Fairbanks), North Pole Winter Carnival (Fairbanks), Oktoberfest (Fairbanks), Tanana Valley/Alaska State Fair (Fairbanks), Southeast Alaska State Fair (Haines), Taku Rondy at Eaglecrest (Juneau), Festival of the North (Ketchikan), Blueberry Festival (Ketchikan), King Crab Festival (Kodiak), Russian New Year and Masquerade Ball (Kodiak), Alaska State Fair (Palmer), Little Norway Festival (Petersburg), Alaska Day Celebration (Sitka), Progress Days (Soldotna), Bachelor Society Ball (Talkeetna), Gold Rush Days (Valdez), International Ice Climbing Festival (Valdez), Winter Carnival (Valdez), Tent City Winter Festival (Wrangell).

Tours: Matanuska River (Anchorage), 26 Glacier Cruise (Anchorage), Fort Yukon (Circle), Denali Dog Tours (Denali National Park and Preserve), Nenana River Float Trips (Denali National Park and Preserve), Tundra Wildlife Tours (Denali National Park and Preserve), Chilkat Bald Eagle Preserve Float Trips (Haines), Kenai Fjords Tours (Seward), White Pass & Yukon Route (Skagway).

Theater: Alaska Experience Theater (Anchorage), Chilkat Center for the Arts (Haines), "Lady Lou Revue" (Juneau), "Cry of the Wild Ram" (Kodiak), Skagway in the Days of '98 With "Soapy Smith" (Skagway).

Alaska possesses much wild, unspoiled territory. The frigid climate is daunting, but settlers there have found a wealth of both vital natural resources and incredible natural beauty. Today, residents struggle to find a balance between developing the resources and preserving the pristine environment.

The Mendenhall Glacier is an ancient sheet of ice that covers an entire valley. Much of Alaska's rugged terrain is inaccessible to man and has never been fully explored.

The Land and the Climate

Alaska is located at the northwesternmost part of the North American continent. It is bordered on the west by the Bering Sea, on the north by the Arctic Ocean, on the east by the Canadian Yukon Territory and the province of British Columbia, and on the south by the Pacific Ocean and the Gulf of Alaska. The state has four main land regions: the Pacific Mountain System, the Central Uplands and Lowlands, the Rocky Mountain System, and the Arctic Coastal Plain.

The Pacific Mountain System is a long, narrow region that extends from the Aleutian Islands in the west to the south coast; it is part of a group of mountain ranges that stretch from Alaska to southern California. The area is filled with ice fields and towering peaks, including 20,320-foot Mount McKinley, the highest point in North America. It also has several active volcanoes. The territory includes two areas of lowlands—the Copper River Basin and the Susitna-Cook Inlet Lowland. It is in the Pacific Mountain System that most of the state's industry and farming are situated. Here are dairy farms, grain fields, and coal mines, as well as oil wells and forest-product factories. Fishing is a big industry off the southern coast.

The Central Uplands and Lowlands comprise the largest land area in Alaska and are located just north of the Pacific Mountain System, running east to west. It is a land of low hills and river valleys, where potatoes and grains flourish. Reindeer, introduced from Siberia, are raised here, and the region contains gold, silver, and antimony mines.

The Rocky Mountain system in Alaska consists of the Brooks Range and its foothills, which form a narrow strip running east and west above the Central Uplands and Lowlands. Some natural gas wells are located here.

The Arctic Coastal Plain runs along the northern border of the state. It is a bleak but beautiful land, treeless because the ground is permanently frozen beneath the topsoil. But in the spring the surface soils thaw and are quickly covered with grasses and wildflowers.

Above:
The Alaskan pipeline, which began operations in 1977, transports oil across the state from Prudhoe Bay in the north to Valdez in the south. The discovery in 1968 of huge offshore oil deposits along the Arctic Slope increased Alaska's prosperity dramatically.

At left:
The Matanuska Valley, northeast of Anchorage, is one of the state's most productive farming areas. With a 120-day growing season and summer sunlight of 19 hours, the valley provides about 80 percent of the food supply for nearby Anchorage and other cities and towns.

Above:
The capital city, Juneau, in southeastern Alaska near the British Columbian border, has a dramatic backdrop of mountains. The state's third largest city, Juneau experienced a population increase of 222 percent in the 1970s, largely as a result of the "oil rush."

At right:
Much of Alaska's land is still wild and unsettled. The mountainous terrain makes road-building difficult, and many of the state's resources remain largely untapped. But these same factors make Alaska one of the last great natural wildlife refuges in the world.

The coastline of Alaska is 6,640 miles long. The state has thousands of lakes, and its most important rivers are the Yukon, the Kuskokwim, the Colville, the Tanana, and the Copper.

Just as Alaska varies enormously in topography, so does it vary in climate. Along the southern coasts and the island groups that flank them, the climate is surprisingly mild, thanks to the Japan Current sweeping in from the west. Rainfall is heavy, in places as high as 150 inches per year. The average winter temperatures are about 32 degrees Fahrenheit, with summer temperatures running from 50 to 60 degrees F.

In the southern coastal valleys, in and around Anchorage, it is cooler and drier, with greater extremes both summer and winter—more like the north-central Plains area of the lower 48 states. The island chain to the west has its own peculiar climate—cool and very foggy year round—pleasant only for its native inhabitants, the herds of seals. In the central valley it is still drier, with winter temperatures often falling to 30 or 40 degrees below zero and summer temperatures soaring above 85 degrees F. The average rainfall in the valley regions is only about 15 to 20 inches per year.

Arctic Alaska on the north is, as its name implies, cold most of the time, with a climate comparable to that of northern Norway. But summer days of almost total daylight in various parts of the Arctic warm up the land, encouraging thousands of delicate flowers to bloom.

The History

When Europeans first arrived in what would become Alaska, three different types of native people were living in this vast area: the Eskimos, the Aleuts, and the Indians. The Eskimos lived in the far north and west, generally near the coast, where they hunted sea mammals and fished. Closely related to the Eskimos were the Aleuts, skillful sea hunters who lived on the Aleutian Islands and the Alaska Peninsula. The Alaskan Indians were hunting and fishing people who varied their diet with edible plant materials that were found in the area, as did the other two groups. The Tlingit and the Haida Indians lived along the south coast, which was also inhabited by the less numerous Tsimshian. In the interior were the Athapaskan tribes.

Most people knew nothing about Alaska until other parts of the western hemisphere had been discovered, named, and settled. Alaska's discovery was made almost by accident. In 1725 Czar Peter the Great of Russia commissioned a Danish navigator named Vitus Bering to find out whether North America and Siberia were connected by land. Bering and his men traveled more than 6,000 miles across Russia and Asia to the Siberian coast, where they built a ship, the *Saint Gabriel*, which finally set sail in 1728.

The expedition sailed through what would be named the Bering Strait between Asia and North America, but could not see the Alaskan mainland because of fog. In 1741 Bering made his second voyage, on which he saw Mount Saint Elias in southeastern Alaska and landed on Kayak Island. Shortly thereafter, Bering died of scurvy, a disease resulting from the lack of Vitamin C, which killed many sailors of his time. But members of his party collected animals from the Alaskan coast and took them back to Russia. They included the sea otter and the fur seal.

Furs were important to Russia, and the pelts brought to the imperial court by Bering's men were among the sleekest, softest, and

English captain James Cook explored and mapped the Alaskan coastline in 1778, six years before the Russians made their settlement on Kodiak Island. During the early 1800s, there was fierce rivalry between fur traders from Russia and the British Hudson's Bay Company. The coastal waters were rich with otter, seal, and other fur-bearing animals, which led to constant boundary disputes.

richest ever seen. So hunters and trappers from Siberia, called *promyshlenniki*, crossed the fog-swept channel that separated Alaska from Siberia and began to slaughter the seals and sea otters. The wealth of furs in Alaska was so great that large Russian companies were formed to exploit it. One of them was responsible for the first European settlement in Alaska, on Kodiak Island, just off the southwest coast, in 1784. Then the Russian government took an official interest and formed the Russian-American Company in 1799. Alexander Baranof was its manager, and he selected a site near present-day Sitka as his headquarters. This company was the only governing power in Alaska for the next 68 years.

Baranof treated the Indians ruthlessly and made slaves of the Aleuts. In 1802 the Tlingit Indians revolted, attacking Sitka and massacring many Russian settlers. The town was rebuilt in 1804, and it remains the most Russian-looking city in North America. From Sitka, the Russian colonists extended their claims and control as far south as California.

Baranof died in 1819, and thereafter Russian interest in Alaska declined. In 1823 the young United States of America proclaimed the Monroe Doctrine, opposing further European colonization or influence in North America, which was aimed in part at the Russian hold on the Northwest. Britain and the United States agreed on zones of influence that limited Russia still more.

While Russia's interest in, and profits from, Alaska diminished, those of the United States increased. The West Coast fishing interests wanted control of Alaskan waters. The Western Union Telegraph Company had a plan to lay a cable to Siberia, and thence to Europe, by way of Alaska. Toward the middle of the 19th century, Russia began to liquidate its North American domain, first selling its California holdings and claims to a Swiss immigrant named John Sutter (it was on his property that gold was discovered in 1848).

International trends came to a climax in 1867, when William H. Seward, the United States Secretary of State in the Andrew Johnson administration, offered Russia $7.2 million for Alaska. The deal was made within a matter of hours (actually, Russia wanted out so badly that it would have settled for $5 million) and was signed at 4:00 A.M. on March 30, 1867. Opponents of the Alaska Purchase labeled it "Seward's Folly," "Seward's Icebox," and "Johnson's Polar Bear Garden."

The American flag went up over Sitka on October 18, 1867, and the entire vast new land was put in charge of a few U.S. Army officers. Then, in 1880, gold was discovered near what is now Juneau, resulting in a small stampede of prospectors. Ironically, it was not this discovery, but rather gold strikes in the Klondike region of Canada to the east, in 1896, that caused the famous rush to Alaska.

U.S. Secretary of State William H. Seward was instrumental in purchasing Alaska from Russia. Seward and his eloquent colleague Charles Sumner endorsed the chance to buy the huge area for $7,200,000—less than two cents per acre. The sale was consummated on March 30, 1867, after months of sharp debate and Congressional opposition. Alaska was referred to at the time as "Seward's Ice Box" and "Seward's Folly."

Sitka was an important commercial center in Russian Alaska at the turn of the 19th century. Founded in 1799 by Siberian merchant Alexander Baranof, it was headquarters for the Russian-American Company, which exploited Alaska's native peoples and wildlife to advance its fur-trading interests.

It was easier to reach the Klondike by way of Alaska than across the rugged wilds of Canada. Some of the prospectors returning from the Canadian Yukon joined the Nome Rush in 1899 and the rush near Fairbanks in 1903. These miners, called sourdoughs for the bread they baked from fermented dough, made headlines all over the world. Few of them made much money from gold, but they created robust and colorful legends. Young writers like Robert Service, Jack London, and Rex Beach made more money recording the exploits of the sourdoughs than most miners made from their claims.

The era of modern Alaska officially began in 1912, with the establishment of local government, preceded by relocation of the capital from Sitka to Juneau in 1906. The hysteria of individual gold prospecting was over. Gold mining had become big business, conducted by great placer mines and dredging. Fishing became more important. Lumber interests began to use the timber from the forests. The Alaskan Railway from Seward to Fairbanks was begun in 1915.

The entry of the United States into World War II in 1941 gave enormous impetus to Alaskan air travel, both civil and military, particularly long-range intercontinental flights. Alaska became the center for shorter routes between the United States and the Orient

and Europe. The territory also became the first line of domestic
defense. Army camps, naval bases, and air bases sprang up. The
1,500-mile Alaska Highway was built to provide a land link.
Thousands of young men, and many of their families, went to Alaska
to help install and man the new bases. Engineers and lumbermen
discovered that Alaska was incredibly rich in natural resources,
including mineral wealth and timber.

In June of 1942, Japanese amphibious forces landed on Agattu,
Attu, and Kiska, in the westernmost Aleutians. The following March
a U.S. naval force defeated the Japanese off the western Aleutians in
the first battle fought in American territory since that of
Appomattox, at the end of the Civil War. Of more than 300,000
military personnel stationed in the area during the war, many stayed,
or returned as civilian citizens.

On January 3, 1959, Alaska became the 49th state of the Union,
with William Egan as its first governor. Ernest Gruening and Edward
Lewis ''Bob'' Bartlett were elected U.S. senators and Ralph J. Rivers
became the U.S. representative.

In 1977 the vast trans-Alaska pipeline was completed. Extending
for 800 miles, it is designed to carry one and a half million barrels of
oil a day from the Arctic shore to the southern port of Valdez.

On March 24, 1989, the largest oil spill in U.S. history occurred
when the Exxon oil tanker *Valdez* struck Bligh Reef in Alaska's Prince
William Sound. It is estimated that 240,000 barrels (11 million gal-
lons) of the 1.26 million barrels of crude oil aboard the ship were
released into the sound. The spill extended for 45 miles and temporar-
ily wiped out the fishing industry, killing many birds and sea life
inhabiting these waters. Exxon assumed full financial responsibility
for the cleanup, but environmentalists accused both the Exxon corpo-
ration and the federal government of a delayed and insufficient
response to this disastrous spill.

Today, Alaska still has problems in trying to develop its huge land
area with a very sparse and widely scattered population. The
expenses of transportation and shipping make the cost of living

Alaskan Indian culture thrives in the southwest corner of the state. Here, members of the Tlingit tribe prepare for a ritual dance in traditional dress. The culture of these Indians, similar to tribes in nearby Canada, is distinctive to the northwest coast of North America.

extremely high, and roads and railroads are difficult to build because of the mountains. But Alaska's hardy people are well suited to the task of developing their wild and beautiful state, which is truly the nation's last frontier.

Education

The first formal school in American Alaska was a girls school founded in 1877 by Amanda McFarland in Wrangell. Later, missionary leader Sheldon Jackson established a system of schools for natives in south-eastern and western Alaska. The first public-school system began in 1912. In the 1970s, the public-school system became responsible for native education. Schools were built in the rural bush areas, but high salaries have been necessary to attract teachers to the area. The United States Bureau of Indian Affairs also operates schools for native children in many villages.

In 1878, Sheldon Jackson established the first institution of higher education in Alaska—Sheldon Jackson College—with the mission of providing vocational and other types of education to Alaskan natives. The Alaska Agricultural College and School of Mines, founded in 1914, in Fairbanks was the second institution of higher education in the state and developed into the University of Alaska.

The People

Approximately 42 percent of the people in Alaska live in metropolitan areas; only about one-third of them were born in the state, and 95 percent were born in the United States. Most of those from other states are members of the U.S. armed forces stationed in this strategic area where North America, Asia, and Europe are in close proximity to one another. The largest religious groups in Alaska are the Roman Catholic, Russian Orthodox, and Protestant communities, including the Baptist, Presbyterian, Methodist, Episcopal, and Lutheran Churches.

Alaska's native peoples are the Eskimos (also known as the Inuit), the Aleuts, the Northwest Coast Indians such as the Tlingit and Haida tribes, and several Athapaskan tribes.

The Eskimos have no tribal groups as such, but they are similarly organized into linguistic and community groups. The family is their primary social unit, and community rules of conduct take the place of strict legal systems among them. Their traditional way of life revolves around the search for food, especially sea animals. The Eskimos have contributed the words igloo, kayak, and parka to the English language, and they are skilled carvers of small objects in bone, ivory, and soapstone. The Northwest Coast Indians of Alaska are expert carvers of wood and stone. Their colorful totem poles and "spirit houses," which ornament their cemeteries, are striking features of the Alaskan landscape. They are also renowned boat builders, weavers, and fishermen.

A wooden mask, *The Mouse Man*, from Tlingit, Alaska.

Famous People

Several famous people were born or relocated to the state of Alaska. Here are a few:

Edward Louis "Bob" Bartlett 1904-68, Washington. Political leader and journalist

Benny Benson 1913-72, Chignik. Designed state flag at age 13

Charles E. Bunnell 1878-1956, Pennsylvania. Educator and first president of the University of Alaska

Captain James B. Cook 1728-1779, England. Leader of first British expedition to map the coast of Alaska

William Healey Dall 1728-1779, ?. Explorer and author: *Alaska and Its Resources*

Anthony Joseph Dimond 1881-1953, New York. Prospector, miner, and judge. Championed Alaskan statehood

Ernest Gruening 1887-1974, New York. Statesman and author: *The State of Alaska* (1954); also led the fight for Alaskan statehood

B. Frank Heintzleman 1888-1965, Pennsylvania. Governor who worked for the economic development of Alaska

Walter J. Hickel b. 1919, Kansas. Governor and U.S. secretary of the interior

Sheldon Jackson 1834-1909, New York. Missionary and educator

Joe Juneau 1826-1900, ?. Prospector and gold miner during the 1880 gold rush

Scott Loucks b. 1956, Anchorage. Baseball player

Alfred P. Swineford 1834-1909, Wisconsin. Politician and journalist.

James Wickersham 1857-1939, Illinois. U.S. district judge and Alaskan delegate to U.S. Congress

Colleges and Universities

There are several colleges and universities in Alaska. Here are the more prominent, with their locations, dates of founding, and enrollments.

Alaska Pacific University, Anchorage, 1957, 379
Sheldon Jackson College, Sitka, 1878, 326
University of Alaska, Anchorage, Anchorage, 1954, 16,720; *Fairbanks*, Fairbanks, 1917, 4,342; *Southeast*, Juneau, 1972, 701

Where To Get More Information

Alaska Division of Tourism
PO Box 110801
Juneau, AK 99811-0801

Idaho

The state seal of Idaho, designed by Emma Edwards Green, was adopted in 1891. In the center of the seal there is a shield, with trees, mountains, farms, and a river representing Idaho's natural beauty. To the left, a woman holding a spear and scales signifies justice; to the right, a miner symbolizes Idaho's vast mineral resources. The state motto appears on a scroll above the shield, and beneath it an elk's head represents the state's wildlife. A sheaf of wheat, two cornucopias, and the state flower appear at the bottom; and a yellow border with "Great Seal of the State of Idaho" encircles the seal.

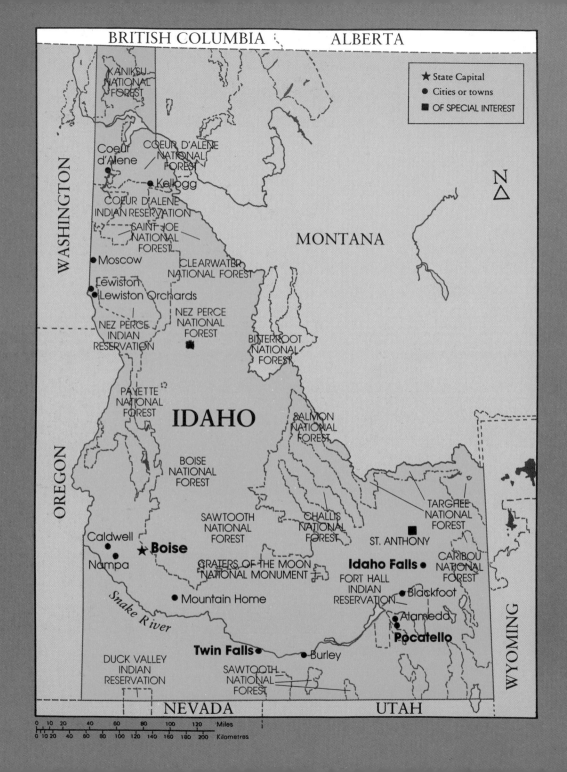

IDAHO
At a Glance

Capital: Boise

Major Industries: Agriculture, livestock, lumbering, mining, electronics

State Flower: Syringa

State Bird: Mountain Bluebird

State Flag

Size: 83,564 square miles (13th largest)
Population: 1,067,250 (42nd largest)

State Flag

The state flag, adopted in 1907, consists of the state seal on a blue field. A red band bordered in gold, with "State of Idaho" written upon it, appears beneath the seal. Gold fringe decorates the edges.

State Motto

Esto Perpetua

This Italian phrase, meaning "It is forever," is a quote from Pietro Sarpi, the Venetian theologian and mathematician.

The 12,000-acre Nez Percé National Historic Park provides visitors with a rich and varied look at both tribal culture and white exploration and settlements.

State Capital

In 1863, when the Idaho Territory was formed, Lewiston was chosen as the capital. Boise became the capital the following year and has remained so ever since.

State Name and Nickname

The name Idaho was originally believed to be a Shoshone word meaning "gem of the mountains." In reality, it had been invented by George M. Willing as a name for the Colorado Territory. When Congress designated the Idaho Territory in 1863, the true origin of the word was still generally unknown.

Idaho is known popularly as the *Gem State,* or *Gem of the Mountains.*

State Flower

The state legislature selected Syringa, *Philadelphus lewisii,* as state flower in 1931.

State Tree

In 1935, the white pine, *Pinus monticola,* was designated state tree.

State Bird

In a vote by school children in 1931, the mountain bluebird, *Sialia currucoides,* was chosen state bird.

State Gem

The star garnet was named state gem in 1967.

State Horse

The Appaloosa was adopted as state horse in 1975.

State Song

"Here We Have Idaho," with music by Sallie Hume Douglas and words by McKinley Helm and Albert J. Tompkins, was designated state song in 1931.

Population

The population of Idaho in 1992 was 1,067,250, making it the 42nd largest state. There are 12.05 people per square mile.

Industries

The principal industries of the state are agriculture, manufacturing, tourism, lumber, mining, and electronics. The chief manufactured products are processed foods, lumber and wood products, chemical products, primary metals, fabricated metal products, machinery, and electronic components.

A dramatic view of Yellowstone National Park.

Agriculture

The chief crops of the state are potatoes, peas, sugar beets, alfalfa seed, wheat, hops, barley, plums and prunes, mint, onions, corn, cherries, apples, and hay. Idaho is also a livestock state. There are estimated to be 1.66 million cattle, 296,000 sheep, 72,000 hogs, and 1.1 million chickens and turkeys on its farms. Yellow and white pine, Douglas fir, and white spruce are harvested. Phosphate rock, silver, gold, sand, and gravel are important mineral products.

Government

The governor of Idaho is elected to a four-year term, as are the lieutenant governor, secretary of state, auditor, treasurer, attorney general, and superintendent of public instruction. The state legislature, which meets annually, consists of a 35-member Senate and a 70-member House of Representatives. Each of the state's 35 legislative districts elects 1 senator and 2 representatives. Senators and representatives serve two-year terms. The most recent constitution was adopted in 1889, eleven months before Idaho became a state. In addition to its two United States senators, the state has two representatives in the U.S. House of Representatives. Idaho has four votes in the electoral college.

Sports

Many sporting events on the collegiate and secondary school levels are played throughout the state. In addition, hunting, fishing, and skiing are also popular pastimes.

Major Cities

Boise (population 125,551). The capital of Idaho, settled in 1862 during the gold rush days, is the state's largest city, as well as its business, financial, and transportation center. Its low cost of living and liberal tax laws have attracted many national and multinational firms, which maintain headquarters here.

Things to see in Boise:
State Capitol, Julia Davis Park, Idaho State Historical Society Museum, Boise City Zoo, Boise Art Museum, Boise Interagency Fire Center, Discovery Center of Idaho, First United Methodist Church (1960), Idaho Botanical Garden, Table Rock, Howard Platt Gardens and Union Pacific Depot, St. Michael's Episcopal Cathedral (1900), Old Idaho Penitentiary (1870), World Center for Birds of Prey, Wild Waters Waterslide Theme Park, Eagle Island State Park, and Lucky Peak State Park.

Pocatello (population 46,117). Founded in 1881 as a tent town along the railroad, this city is a major junction between Omaha, Nebraska, and Portland, Oregon. Originally part of the Fort Hall Indian Reservation, it was named for the Bannock Indian chief who gave the Utah & Northern Railroad the right of way to build a Salt Lake City-to-Butte rail line. The second largest city in

Idaho, it is the home of about 50 manufacturing plants, including electronic components, steel, cement, mining machinery, cheese products, and phosphorus.

Things to see in Pocatello: Idaho Museum of Natural History, Bannock County Historical Museum, Ross Park, Old Fort Hall Replica, and Standrod House.

Places to Visit

The National Park Service maintains three areas in the state of Idaho: Craters of the Moon National Monument, Yellowstone National Park, and Nez Percé National Historical Park. In addition, there are 18 state recreation areas.

Arco: Experimental Breeder Reactor Number 1. Visitors may tour nuclear reactors and a reactor control room at the site of the first atomic reactor to generate electricity.

Blackfoot: Bingham County Historical Museum. This restored 1905 homestead contains a gun collection, Indian relics, and antique furniture.

Buhl: Balanced Rock. This 40-foot-high tower of rock resembles a mushroom cloud from an atomic bomb.

Coeur d'Alene: Silverwood. This turn-of-the-century mining town theme park features an antique airplane museum, a wild animal exhibit, and rides.

Kellogg: Old Mission State Park. This park contains the Coeur d'Alene Mission of the Sacred Heart, a restored Indian mission and the oldest building in the state.

Lewiston: Castle Museum. This three-story house, built in 1906 of handmade cement blocks, was modeled after a Scottish castle.

Montpelier: Minnetonka Cave. The cave, which lies at 7,700 feet above sea level, contains fossils of plants and marine animals from a prehistoric sea.

Moscow: Appaloosa Horse Museum. This museum features exhibits and artifacts relating to the Appaloosa horse, as well as cowboy and Nez Percé Indian memorabilia.

Salmon: Lemhi. This historic ghost town, named for a character in *The Book of Mormon*, was built in 1855.

Sandpoint: Vintage Wheel Museum. The antique car

collection housed at this museum includes a Stanley Steamer and a 1913 Cadillac.

Shoshone: Shoshone Indian Ice Caves. These caves, which maintain a constant temperature of 30-33 degrees Fahrenheit, contain beautiful ice formations.

Wallace: Northern Pacific Depot Railroad Museum. The first floor of this restored station contains a re-creation of an early 1900s railroad depot, as well as railroad memorabilia.

Weiser: Fiddlers Hall of Fame. This museum features a collection of old time fiddles.

Events

There are many events and organizations that schedule activities of various kinds in the state of Idaho. Here are some of them.

Sports: Horse racing at Les Bois Park (Boise), River Super Float (Boise), Burley Speedboat Regatta (Burley), Little Britches Rodeo (Caldwell), War Bonnet Roundup (Idaho Falls), horse racing at the Jerome County Fairgrounds (Jerome), Chariot Races (Jerome), NAIA World Series Baseball Tournament (Lewiston), Regional Hydroplane Races (Lewiston), Jet Boat Race (Lewiston), Snake

River Stampede (Nampa), Frontier Rodeo (Pocatello), Pacific Northwest Sled Dog Championship Races (Priest Lake), International Draft Horse Show and Sale (Sandpoint), Sandpoint Winter Carnival (Sandpoint), Duchin Celebrity Invitational Cup (Sun Valley), Western Days (Twin Falls).

Arts and Crafts: Art on the Green (Coeur d'Alene), Gem Dandy Days (Jerome), Arts in the Park (Shoshone), Sun Valley Center Arts and Crafts Fair (Sun Valley).

Music: American Festival Ballet (Boise), Boise Philharmonic (Boise), Jazzfest (Coeur d'Alene), Music Festival (McCall), Lionel Hampton/Chevron Jazz Festival (Moscow), Summer Band Concert Series (Pocatello), Idaho International Folk Dance Festival (Rexburg), Old Time Fiddlers' Jamboree (Shoshone), Sun Valley Music Festival (Sun Valley), National Oldtime Fiddlers' Contest (Weiser).

Entertainment: Massacre Rocks Rendezvous (American Falls), Eastern Idaho State Fair (Blackfoot), Old Boise Days (Boise), Western Idaho State Fair (Boise), Harvestfest (Buhl), Sagebrush Days (Buhl), Cassia County Fair and Rodeo (Burley), Canyon County Fair (Caldwell), Oktoberfest (Coeur d'Alene), North Idaho Fair (Coeur d'Alene), Shoshone-Bannock Indian Festival (Fort Hall), Winter Festival (Grangeville), Jerome County Fair (Jerome), Septemberfest (Kellogg), Rendezvous-Pioneer Days Celebration (Lava Hot Springs), Dogwood Festival (Lewiston), Lewiston Air Fair (Lewiston), Lewiston Roundup (Lewiston), Nez Percé County Fair (Lewiston), Winter Carnival (McCall), Bear Lake County Fair and Rodeo (Montpelier), Moscow Mardi Gras and Beaux Arts Ball (Moscow), Latah County Fair (Moscow), Rendezvous in the Park (Moscow), Clearwater County Fair and Lumberjack Days (Orofino), Minidoka County Fair and Rodeo (Rupert), Fremont County Pioneer Days (St. Anthony), Paul Bunyan Days (St. Maries), Salmon River Day (Salmon), Festival at Sandpoint (Sandpoint), Lincoln County Fair (Shoshone), Wagon Days (Sun Valley), Twin Falls County Fair and Rodeo (Twin Falls).

Tours: Boise Tour Train (Boise), Hells Canyon Excursions (Lewiston), Barker-Ewing River Trips (Salmon), Sierra Silver Mine Tour (Wallace), jet boat tours (Weiser).

Theater: Morrison Center for the Performing Arts (Boise), Idaho Shakespeare Festival (Boise), Idaho Repertory Theater (Moscow).

The Wagon Days Parade, held over the Labor Day weekend in Ketchum, Idaho, is the largest non-motorized parade in the west. The parade originated in the 1950s, in celebration of Ketchum's mining heritage.

Above:
At Shoshone Falls, in southern Idaho, the Snake River tumbles 212 feet over a sheer cliff to form one of the nation's greatest waterfalls.

Above right:
The mighty Snake River, more than 1,000 miles long, flows west across southern Idaho and then north to become part of the state's western border. Between Idaho and Oregon, it slashes through the rock of Hells Canyon to create the deepest cut on the North American continent.

The Land and the Climate

The shape of Idaho is curious. The southern part is a rectangle 310 miles east to west, 175 miles north to south. But the upper part is a narrowing panhandle only 45 miles wide at the northern end, where it abuts the Canadian province of British Columbia. The western border, divided between Washington and Oregon, is 483 miles north to south. South of the ruler-straight southern border are the states of Nevada and Utah. In the east, the winding state line is shared with Wyoming and Montana. Idaho has three major land regions: the Rocky Mountains Region, the Columbia Plateau, and the Basin and Range Region.

The Rocky Mountains Region is Idaho's largest, covering the panhandle, forming a bow down three-quarters of the state, and on the east forming a strip along the Wyoming border. This region includes some of the most rugged areas in the United States. Parts of it can be explored only on foot or on horseback. Plateaus, valleys, mountains, canyons, and gorges typify this area. In the valleys there are wheat and pea farms, with some hog and beef ranches. It is a land of natural resources, where forest products are harvested and gold, copper, zinc, lead, thorium, mercury, uranium, and silver are mined.

The Columbia Plateau runs parallel to the Snake River in southern Idaho, then curves north along the western border. It has fertile valleys where sugar beets, potatoes, alfalfa, beans, and other crops are grown on irrigated land. This is also a region of cattle and sheep ranches.

The Basin and Range Region is in the southeastern part of the state. Its mountains alternate with deep valleys and grassy plains. Cattle, sheep, and wheat are raised here.

Idaho has more than 50 mountains that rise higher than 10,000 feet above sea level. The highest mountain in the state, Borah Peak, reaches 12,662 feet. Idaho's most important rivers are the Snake, the Salmon, the Columbia, the Kootenai, and the Spokane. There are mineral springs in Idaho, and many spectacular waterfalls. Idaho has more than 2,000 explored lakes, but geographers estimate that there are hundreds more that have not been discovered.

Idaho's climate is of the dry continental type, quite cold in winter, often very hot in summer. Lack of humidity, and prevailing west winds from the Pacific Ocean, give the most populated areas an ideal four-season climate. Annual rainfall ranges from 8 to 20 inches, and winter snowfall in the mountains varies from 40 to 100 inches.

Below left:
Bogus Basin, in southeastern Idaho, forms a dramatic snow-covered landscape. The state's mountainous terrain has made it a favorite with skiers. Sun Valley, in the Sawtooth Mountains, is an internationally famous resort.

Below:
Idaho potatoes, famous for their outstanding flavor, are the state's best-known crop. By the early 1980s, Idaho was producing more than a quarter of all the potatoes grown in the United States.

A view of Idaho's stunning landscape. The state has more than 50 mountains that rise higher than 10,000 feet above sea level. The terrain is so rugged that some parts of Idaho can be explored only on foot or on horseback.

The History

There were people living in what would become Idaho more than 10,000 years ago. These Paleo-Indians are known through archaeological finds, including paintings and carvings on rocks, called petroglyphs. When Canadians and Americans arrived, they found members of the Nez Percé, Coeur d'Alene, Pend d'Oreille, Shoshone, Kutenai, and Bannock tribes. The wilderness teemed with fur-bearing animals, fish, and game.

Meriwether Lewis and William Clark were probably the first non-Indians to explore the Idaho region, during their expedition through the lands of the Louisiana Purchase. They crossed the huge Bitterroot Range in 1805 and floated down the Clearwater and Snake Rivers to the west's greatest river, the Columbia. Their reports of innumerable fur-bearing animals brought the trappers, and in 1809 a Canadian explorer, David Thompson, set up a trading post at Pend Oreille Lake. Later, in 1834, Fort Boise and Fort Hall were built to compete against each other for the fur trade.

The first white settlers in Idaho were two Presbyterian missionaries, Henry H. Spalding and his wife. They organized the Lapwai Mission Station, near present-day Lewiston, in 1836. In 1855 a group of Mormons began farming in the eastern part of the area and built Fort Lemhi, but they were forced out by Indian

Below:
Covered wagons were the primary means of transportation for pioneers who settled the Northwest. Many traveled the rugged Oregon Trail, which ran across southern Idaho.

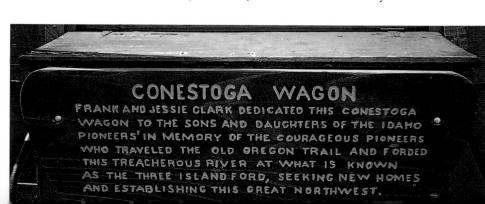

CONESTOGA WAGON
FRANK AND JESSIE CLARK DEDICATED THIS CONESTOGA WAGON TO THE SONS AND DAUGHTERS OF THE IDAHO PIONEERS' IN MEMORY OF THE COURAGEOUS PIONEERS WHO TRAVELED THE OLD OREGON TRAIL AND FORDED THIS TREACHEROUS RIVER AT WHAT IS KNOWN AS THE THREE ISLAND FORD, SEEKING NEW HOMES AND ESTABLISHING THIS GREAT NORTHWEST.

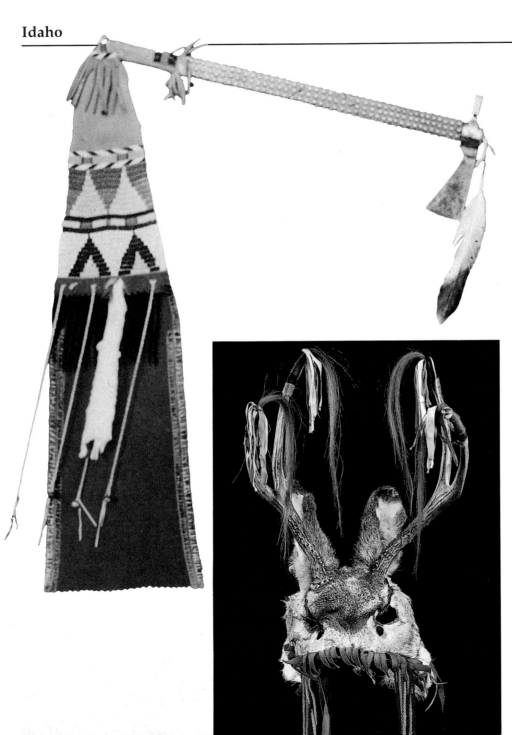

At left:
A Shoshone tomahawk, decorated with beadwork and feathers.

Below left:
The Shoshone Indians were among the first inhabitants of the Idaho region. Their clothing, elaborate headdresses, and other accessories were made from the skins, bones, feathers, and fur of the animals that were found in the area.

Chief Joseph led his people in the Nez Percé War of 1877, when the federal government attempted to settle them on Idaho's Lapwai Reservation from their Oregon lands in the Wallowa Valley. Joseph and his followers won the Battle of White Bird Canyon in north-central Idaho, then conducted a fighting retreat toward the Canadian border against superior government forces. In October 1877, they were finally forced to surrender, and Joseph, moved by his people's suffering, vowed, "I will fight no more forever."

attacks. In 1860 a new party of Mormons arrived and founded Idaho's first permanent white settlement at Franklin.

Most Americans paid little attention to remote Idaho until gold was discovered on Orofino Creek in the Clearwater country in 1860, followed by rich strikes in the Salmon River and Florence areas, the Boise Basin, and Coeur d'Alene. Gold seekers poured into the Idaho region, but after the mines had been exhausted, the gold camps became ghost towns. Farmers and ranchers, however, had come to the area to feed the miners, and the agriculture and livestock industries had begun.

In 1863 the Idaho Territory was established, with Lewiston as its capital. This territory included present-day Idaho, Montana, and almost all of Wyoming. Later, Montana (in 1864) and Wyoming (in 1868) became separate territories. The capital of the Idaho Territory was moved to Boise in 1864.

The 1870s brought fierce Indian wars to Idaho. In 1877 the Nez Percé War broke out when the United States Army tried to force this tribe to move onto the Lapwai Reservation in Idaho. Under the leadership of Chief Joseph, the Nez Percé revolted, crushing army troops in a battle at White Bird Canyon in north-central Idaho on June 17. But the Indians were forced to retreat when more U.S. soldiers were brought into action. Chief Joseph surrendered in October 1877 near the Canadian border.

The Bannock Indians rebelled in 1877 and 1878, because food was scarce on their reservation and they had lost their traditional hunting grounds to settlers. When they began to dig roots for food from the prairie, the cattle ranchers objected and the army was called in. A war broke out, but when the Bannock chief Buffalo Horn was killed, the Indians surrendered.

It was in 1890 that Idaho entered the Union as the 43rd state. Still, it wasn't until the end of the 19th century that the trickle of settlers became a steady flow. Rich silver and lead deposits were found, and a railroad managed to thread the mountain gorges and tunnel through the peaks.

Sheep raising became an important agricultural product in Idaho in the years leading up to World War I.

During the 1890s violence erupted between the miners and mine owners, and between union and nonunion miners. The Coeur d'Alene region was the scene of dynamiting and shooting until the U.S. Army was called in to enforce a peace. In the years that followed, lumbering and sheep raising became more widespread. The volcanic soil of the Snake River Valley in the south was good for crops, and extensive farming, aided by irrigation, began.

When the United States entered World War I in 1917, Idaho's agriculture began to boom. But the state's farmers tended to overexpand, and after the war, while the rest of the country enjoyed prosperity, they were in debt and hard pressed to make a living. Then, oddly enough, recovery began during the Great Depression of the 1930s, when farmers moved in from the drought-ridden Great Plains, having discovered that Idaho's farmlands were still productive.

World War II brought more boom times to the state. Idaho's agricultural products were in great demand, and state factories made arms, munitions, and airplanes. After the war, the national housing boom spurred Idaho's lumber industry. The first nuclear reactors for generating electricity by atomic energy were built in Arco in the 1950s. In 1976, the new Teton Dam on the Snake River collapsed, killing 11 people and causing a large amount of property damage. This disaster prompted a greater concern for environmental protection.

Today, the population of Idaho is shifting from rural areas to cities and towns, as the state becomes more industrialized and diversified. The lumber industry, for example, is now manufacturing such wood and paper products as prefabricated houses, boxes, paper cups, and other items. Tourism has become an important source of revenue. In 1989, out-of-state tourists spent $1.4 billion in Idaho. Improved transportation has made Idaho more accessible and opened up new markets for its products.

Education

Missionary Henry Spalding and his wife opened a school at Lapwai Mission upon their arrival in 1836. When Idaho became a state in 1890, 1,280 acres in each township were set aside for the support of schools and more than 400 common schools were in operation. The first institution of higher education in Idaho was the University of Idaho, established in 1889, one year before statehood.

The People

Roughly 20 percent of Idahoans live in metropolitan areas. About 97 percent of them were born in the United States. Most of the residents of Idaho are descendants of early English, Irish, and Scottish settlers from the eastern and midwestern states, but Japanese, Scandinavians, Germans, Spaniards from the Basque province, and Canadians are also represented. The Mormons are the largest single religious group in the state. Other major denominations include the Roman Catholic, Methodist, Lutheran, Episcopalian, and Presbyterian.

Famous People

Many famous people were born in the state of Idaho. Here are a few:

Ezra Taft Benson, 1899-1994, Whitney. Secretary of agriculture and president of the Church of Jesus Christ of Latter-Day Saints

Gutzon Borglum 1867-1941, near Bear Lake. Sculptor: Mount Rushmore National Monument

Frank Church 1924-84, Boise. Senate leader

Ken Dayley b. 1959, Jerome. Baseball pitcher

Larry Jackson 1931-90, Nampa. Baseball pitcher

William M. Jardine 1879-1955, Oneida County. Secretary of Agriculture

Kamaiakan 1800-80, near Lewiston. Indian leader

Harmon Killebrew b. 1936, Payette. Hall of Fame baseball player

Vance Law b. 1956, Boise. Baseball player

Vern Law b. 1930, Meridian. Baseball pitcher

Ezra Pound 1885-1972, Hailey. Poet and critic: *Homage to Sextus Propertius, Hugh Selwyn Mauberley*

James Rainwater 1917-86, Council. Nobel Prize-winning physicist

Sacagawea 1787-1812, ?. Shoshone interpreter

Lana Turner b. 1920, Wallace. Film actress: *The Postman Always Rings Twice, Peyton Place*

Herman Welker 1906-57, Cambridge. Senate leader

Larry Wilson b. 1938, Rigby. Football player

Colleges and Universities

There are several colleges and universities in Idaho. Here are the more prominent, with their locations, dates of founding, and enrollments.

Albertson College, Caldwell, 1891, 734

Boise State University, Boise, 1932, 11,155

Idaho State University, Pocatello, 1901, 9,020

Lewis-Clark State College, Lewiston, 1955, 3,029

Northwest Nazarene College, Nampa, 1913, 1,186

University of Idaho, Moscow, 1889, 7,467

Where To Get More Information

Idaho Travel Council
700 W. State St., 2nd floor
Boise, ID 83720
1-800-635-7820

Oregon

The state seal of Oregon, adopted in 1903, contains a shield partially encircled by 33 stars and topped by the American Eagle. Pictured on the shield are mountains, forests, an elk, a covered wagon with a team of oxen, the sun setting over the Pacific Ocean, a departing British warship, and an arriving American merchant ship. The last two represent the end of British rule and the rise of American power. A ribbon inscribed with "The Union" divides the shield, and a sheaf of wheat, a plow, and a pickax below the ribbon symbolize agriculture and mining. The border around the seal reads "State of Oregon" and "1859"—the year of the state's admission to the Union.

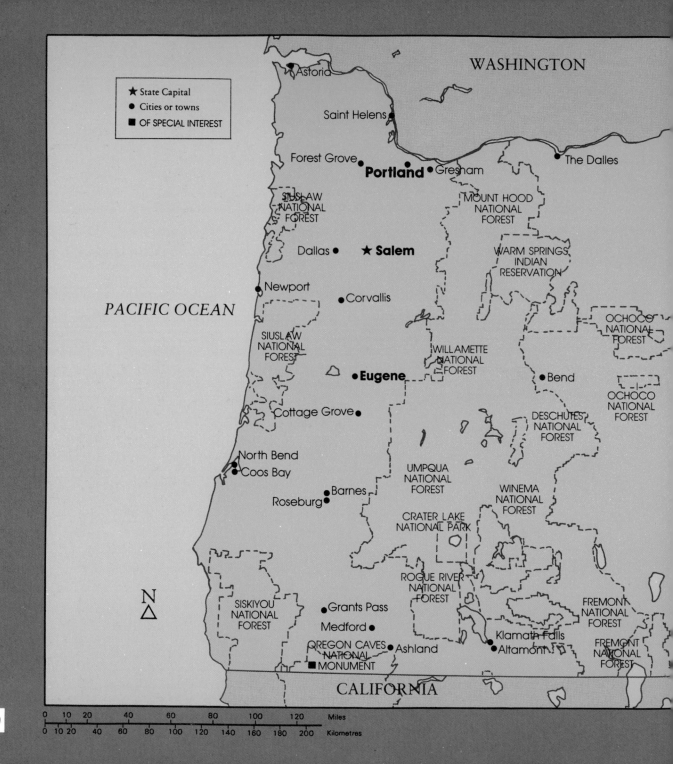

WASHINGTON

★ State Capital
● Cities or towns
■ OF SPECIAL INTEREST

Astoria

Saint Helens

The Dalles

Forest Grove

Portland ● Gresham

SIUSLAW NATIONAL FOREST

MOUNT HOOD NATIONAL FOREST

WARM SPRINGS INDIAN RESERVATION

Dallas ● ★ **Salem**

Newport

Corvallis

PACIFIC OCEAN

SIUSLAW NATIONAL FOREST

OCHOCO NATIONAL FOREST

WILLAMETTE NATIONAL FOREST

Eugene

● Bend

OCHOCO NATIONAL FOREST

Cottage Grove

DESCHUTES NATIONAL FOREST

North Bend

Coos Bay

UMPQUA NATIONAL FOREST

WINEMA NATIONAL FOREST

Barnes

Roseburg

CRATER LAKE NATIONAL PARK

SISKIYOU NATIONAL FOREST

N
△

Grants Pass

ROGUE RIVER NATIONAL FOREST

FREMONT NATIONAL FOREST

Medford

Klamath Falls

OREGON CAVES NATIONAL MONUMENT

Ashland

Altamont

FREMONT NATIONAL FOREST

CALIFORNIA

50

| 0 10 20 | 40 | 60 | 80 | 100 | 120 | Miles |
| 0 10 20 | 40 | 60 | 80 | 100 | 120 | 140 | 160 | 180 | 200 | Kilometres |

OREGON
At a Glance

Capital: Salem

State Flag:

State Bird:
Western Meadowlark

State Flower: Oregon Grape

Major Industries: Forest products, machinery, agriculture, livestock

Size: 97,073 square miles (10th largest)
Population: 2,977,331 (29th largest)

Hermiston

Pendleton

UMATILLA NATIONAL FOREST

UMATILLA INDIAN RESERVATION

La Grande

WALLOWA-WHITMAN NATIONAL FOREST

UMATILLA NATIONAL FOREST

UMATILLA NATIONAL FOREST

Baker

WALLOWA-WHITMAN NATIONAL FOREST

PICTURE GORGE

MALHEUR NATIONAL FOREST

IDAHO

Ontario

OREGON

HART MOUNTAIN NATIONAL ANTELOPE REFUGE

FORT MCDERMITT INDIAN RESERVATION

NEVADA

State Flag

The state flag of Oregon consists of the shield and stars from the state seal printed in gold on a navy blue background. "State of Oregon" appears above the shield and "1859" is inscribed below it. The reverse side contains a picture of a beaver, Oregon's state animal. The flag is sometimes trimmed with gold fringe.

State Motto

She Flies with Her Own Wings

This motto, adopted in 1987, was originally printed on the territorial seal in Latin. It replaces *The Union*, which had been designated in 1957.

Crater Lake, created by an eruption of Mount Mazama, was made a national park in 1902.

State Capital

Salem has been the capital of Oregon since 1855, four years before statehood.

State Name and Nicknames

There are several theories concerning the origin of the name Oregon. French Canadians used the word *ouragon*, meaning "storm" or "hurricane," in connection with the Columbia River, which they often called "the river of storms." The name may have been derived from either of two Spanish words—*orejon*, meaning "big ear," used in reference to the tribes of the region, or *oregano*, because of the abundance of wild sage growing in the area.

Officially, Oregon is known as the *Beaver State* because of the importance of fur trapping in the state's history. The state has also been referred to as the *Web-foot State* for its abundant rainfall, and the *Hard-case State* for the many hardships encountered by the early settlers.

State Flower

The Oregon grape, *Berberis aquifolium*, was selected by the state legislature as state flower in 1899.

State Tree

The Douglas fir, *Pseudotsuga menziessii*, was chosen state tree in 1939.

State Bird

In 1927, the western meadowlark, *Sturnella neglecta*, was proclaimed state bird by the governor after a vote by the state's school children.

State Animal

The American Beaver, *Castor canadensis*, was designated state animal in 1969.

State Dance

The square dance was chosen by the state legislature as official state dance in 1977.

State Fish

The Chinook salmon, *Oncorhynchus tshawytscha*, was selected as state fish in 1961.

State Gemstone

The Oregon sunstone, a large, brightly colored, transparent gem, was declared official state gemstone by the 1987 legislature.

State Insect

The Oregon Swallowtail butterfly, *Papilio oregonius*, was adopted as state insect in 1979.

State Rock

In 1965, the thunderegg, or geode, was chosen state rock.

State Song

"Oregon, My Oregon," with words by J. A. Buchanan and music by Henry B. Murtagh, was designated state song in 1927.

Population

The population of Oregon in 1992 was 2,977,331, making it the 29th most populous state. There are 28.89 people per square mile—68 percent of the population live in metropolitan areas, many of them in the Willamette Valley in such cities as Portland and Salem. About 95 percent of Oregonians were born in the United States, many of them tracing their ancestry back to settlers who came in on the Oregon Trail. Of those born in other nations, most came from Canada and the Scandinavian countries. The majority of Oregon's churchgoers are Protestants—Baptists, Disciples of Christ, Episcopalians, Lutherans, Methodists, Mormons, and Presbyterians. But the largest single religious body consists of Roman Catholics.

Industries

The principal industries of Oregon are forestry, agriculture, manufacturing, tourism, printing and publishing, and high technology. The chief manufactured goods are lumber and wood products, foods, machinery, fabricated metals, paper, and primary metals.

Agriculture

The chief crops of the state are hay, grass seed, farm forest products, wheat, potatoes, onions, and pears. Oregon is also a livestock state. There are estimated to be 1.5 million cattle, 80,000 hogs and pigs, 466,000 sheep, and 3 million chickens and turkeys on its farms. Douglas fir, hemlock, and ponderosa pine are harvested. Crushed stone and construction sand and gravel are important mineral products. Commercial fishing earned $76.2 million in 1992.

Government

The governor is elected to a four-year term, as are the attorney general, labor commissioner, secretary of state, superintendent of public instruction, and treasurer. The state legislature, which meets in odd-numbered years, consists of a 30-member senate and a 60-member house of representatives. Each of the 30 senatorial districts elects one senator to a four-year term, and each of the 60 representative districts elects one representative to a two-year term. The most recent constitution was adopted in 1857, two years prior to statehood. In addition to its two United States senators, Oregon has five representatives in the U.S. House of Representatives. The state has seven votes in the electoral college.

Sports

Many sporting events on the collegiate and secondary school levels are played throughout the state. In football, the University of Oregon won the Rose Bowl in 1917, and Oregon State University won in 1942. The University of Oregon also won the first N.C.A.A. basketball tournament in 1939.

Rick Adelman guided the Portland Trail Blazers to the NBA Finals during the 1989-90 season, his first full season as head coach.

On the professional level, the Portland Trail Blazers of the National Basketball Association play their home games in Memorial Coliseum.

Major Cities

Portland (population 438,802). Founded in 1844 by Asa Lovejoy and William Overton. Overton sold his portion to Francis Pettygrove and in 1845 it was platted as a town. The name was determined by the flip of a coin; Pettygrove won and chose the name of his hometown in Maine, Portland. This pioneer town grew steadily, and by the turn of the century it had become a thriving metropolis. It was an important supply and trading center during the Indian wars of the 1850s and the gold rush. Located on the banks of the Willamette River, Oregon's largest city is a busy port, visited by more than 1,400 ships each year. The surrounding area is famous for its farms, orchards, dairies, and timberlands.

Things to see in Portland: American Advertising Museum, Audubon Society of Portland, Children's Museum, Crystal Springs Rhododendron Gardens, The Grotto, Hoyt Arboretum, Ira Keller Fountain, James F. Bybee House (1858), John Palmer House, Leach Botanical Park, Maveety Gallery, Old Church, Oregon Art Institute, Oregon Historical Society, Oregon Maritime Center and Museum, Oregon Museum of Science and Industry, Peninsula Rose Garden, Pittock Mansion (1914), Portland Police Historical Museum, Washington Park, Washington Park Zoo, and World Forestry Center.

Salem (population 107,793). Oregon's capital was settled in 1840 by missionary Jason Lee, who tried to teach the Indians farming as well as religion. Eventually, Lee founded the Oregon Institute, which became the present-day Willamette University. Today, the state government, food processing, and light manufacturing form the basis of Salem's economy.

Things to see in Salem: Bush's Pasture Park, Bush Barn Art Center, Bush Conservatory, Bush House Museum, Deepwood Estate, Enchanted Forest, Mission Mill Village, Jason Lee House, Parsonage, John D. Boon Home, Thomas Kay Woolen Mill (1889), Silver Falls State Park, and the State Capitol.

Places to Visit

The National Park Service maintains five areas in the state of Oregon: Crater Lake National Park, John Day Fossil Beds National Monument, Oregon Caves National Monument, McLoughlin House National Historic Site, and Fort Clatsop National Memorial. In addition, there are 90 state recreation areas.

Astoria: Columbia River Maritime Museum. This museum features exhibits relating to the history of the Columbia River and the northwest.

Bandon: West Coast Game Park. One of the west coast's largest animal petting parks features more than 450 animals on 21 acres.

Bend: High Desert Museum. Indoor/outdoor exhibits feature live animals, plants, and historical artifacts of the northwest desert region.

Brownsville: Living Rock Studios. In addition to oil paintings and a mineral collection, the studios also contain Biblical scenes portrayed in rock and wood carvings.

The Wallowa Mountains, part of Oregon's many breathtaking mountain ranges.

A 15-inch Brazilian Bahian doll, one of the beautiful collection at the Dolly Wares Museum.

Cottage Grove: Cottage Grove Historical Museum. The museum is housed in an octagonal structure which was built in 1897 as a Catholic church.

Eugene: Willamette Science and Technology Center. Hands-on exhibits explore physics, biology, and computer science.

Florence: Dolly Wares Doll Museum. This museum houses a collection of more than 2,500 dolls from around the world.

Gold Hill: The Oregon Vortex. Strange magnetic forces cause mysterious effects, such as preventing visitors from standing erect.

John Day: Kam Wah Chung & Co. Museum. Originally built in the 1860s as a doctor's office, this museum includes a collection of more than 1,000 herbs and medicines used by an herbal doctor.

Lakeview: Hart Mountain National Antelope Refuge. This 275,000-acre refuge is home to pronghorn antelope, bighorn sheep, and golden eagles, as well as numerous other wildlife species.

Newberg: Hoover-Minthorn House Museum. Built in 1881, this memorial museum contains mementoes of the five years that Herbert Hoover spent here during his childhood.

Newport: Undersea Gardens. Large underwater windows provide visitors with views of marine animals and plants in their natural setting.

Port Orford: Prehistoric Gardens. Visitors can view life-size replicas of dinosaurs in a rain forest setting.

Redmond: Petersen's Rock Gardens. Replicas of famous structures are fashioned out of rock and petrified wood in a colorful setting.

Roseburg: Wildlife Safari. In addition to a drive-through park, this attraction features a petting zoo, animal shows, and elephant rides.

Seal Rock: Sea Gulch. Among the features to be found in this western theme park are over 400 chainsaw-sculpted human and animal figures.

The Dalles: Wonder Works Children's Museum. This museum features many hands-on exhibits, including a child-size space shuttle.

Tillamook: Pioneer Museum. This museum contains exhibits on various aspects of pioneer and Indian life.

Events

There are many events and organizations that schedule activities of various kinds in the state of Oregon. Here are some of them.

Sports: Rodeo and Race Meet (Burns), Columbia River Gorge Sailpark (Hood River), Cross Channel Swim (Hood River), Jordan Valley Rodeo (Jordan Valley), Chief Joseph Days Rodeo (Joseph), auto racing at Portland International Raceway (Portland), auto racing at Portland Speedway (Portland), Cascade Run-Off (Portland), greyhound racing at Multnomah

Kennel Club (Portland), horseracing at Portland Meadows (Portland), Hot Air Balloon Classic (Portland), Indy Car World Series Race (Portland), Portland Marathon (Portland).

Arts and Crafts: Scandinavian Midsummer Festival (Astoria), Artquake Festival (Portland), Central Oregon Art Festival (Prineville), Salem Art Fair and Festival (Salem), East Linn Museum Quilt Show (Sweet Home), Arts and Crafts Fair (Yachats).

Music: The Oregon Coast Music Festival (Coos Bay), Bach Festival (Eugene), All-Northwest Barber Shop Ballad Contest and Gay Nineties Festival (Forest Grove), Bluegrass Festival (Hillsboro), Oregon Symphony Orchestra (Portland), Portland Opera Association (Portland), Rose City Blues Festival (Portland).

Entertainment: World Championship Timber Carnival (Albany), Winter Food (Ashland), Great Astoria Crab Feed and Seafood Festival (Astoria), Cranberry Festival (Bandon), Azalea Festival (Brookings), Beachcombers' Festival (Brookings), Pioneer Picnic (Brownsville), Harney County Fair (Burns), High Desert Hot Air Balloon Rally and Fiddle Contest (Burns), Obsidian Days (Burns), Waterfowl Festival (Burns), Sandcastle Contest (Cannon Beach), "62" Day Celebration (Canyon City), Sternwheeler Days (Cascade Locks), Da Vinci Days (Corvallis), Fleet of Flowers (Depoe Bay), Historic Preservation Week (Eugene), Rhododendron Festival (Florence), Peter Britt Festivals (Jacksonville), Kam Wah Chung Days (John Day), Oregon Trail Days (La Grande), Union County Fair (La Grande), Lake County Fair and Round-Up (Lakeview), Lebanon Strawberry Festival (Lebanon), Jefferson County Fair and Rodeo (Madras), Turkey-Rama (McMinnville), Pear Blossom Festival (Medford), Old-Fashioned Festival (Newberg), Loyalty Days and Sea Fair Festival (Newport), Japanese Obon Festival (Ontario), Malheur County Fair (Ontario), Ontario Winter Wonderland Parade (Ontario), Pendleton Round-Up (Pendleton), Frolic and Rodeo Festival (Philomath), Mount Hood Festival (Portland), Multnomah County Fair (Portland), Neighborfair (Portland), Pacific International Livestock Show (Portland), Portland Oktoberfest (Portland), Rose Festival (Portland), A Taste of Portland (Portland), "Wintering-In" (Portland), Rockhound Pow Wow (Prineville), Oregon State Fair (Salem), West Salem Waterfront Festival (Salem), Broiler Festival (Springfield), Christmas Parade (Springfield), Smelt Fry (Yachats).

Tours: Crater Lake Boat Tour (Crater Lake National Park), Snake River Boat Trips (Hells Canyon National Recreation Area), Oregon Caves tour (Oregon Caves National Monument), Victorian Home Tours (The Dalles).

Theater: Oregon Shakespeare Festival (Ashland), Linfield Little Theater (McMinnville), Dolores Winningstad Theater (Portland), Intermediate Theater (Portland), Portland Center for the Performing Arts (Portland), Willamette Center (Portland).

Green Lakes Basin is one of the state's most popular hiking areas.

In 1843, a large wagon train left Missouri and followed the Oregon Trail to settle in Oregon. From that point on, settlers streamed into the state to take advantage of the rich farms, forests, and fur trade. By the late 1800s, Oregon was linked to the East by railroads, further increasing the population.

The Land and the Climate

Above:
Smith Rock State Park is typical of the rough terrain in much of central Oregon, where ancient volcanic activity created dramatic peaks and valleys.

Below:
Winchester Bay is on the state's Pacific coast, which offers great scenic variety. The Oregon shoreline ranges from wide beaches and sand dunes to sheer rocky cliffs that rise abruptly from the sea.

Oregon is bounded on the west by the Pacific Ocean, on the north by Washington, on the east by Idaho, and on the south by California and Nevada. The state has six main land regions, which are the Coast Range, the Willamette Lowland, the Cascade Mountains, the Klamath Mountains, the Columbia Plateau, and the Basin and Range Region.

The Coast Range runs along the Pacific coast from the northwest corner of the state to the Klamath Mountains in the southwest. This is an area of low mountain ranges and evergreen forests. There are several valleys in the region, and along much of the coast, sheer cliffs rise from the ocean. It is an area of fruit and walnut orchards, dairy and poultry farms, and lumbering operations.

The Willamette Lowland is a narrow strip east of the Coast Range, running about halfway down the state. This is a region of gently rolling farmland with many forests. Rich soil and a favorable climate make it the most important farming area in Oregon, and good water transportation facilities make it the state's most important manufacturing region as well.

The Cascade Mountains dominate a broad belt of rugged land with their volcanic peaks, which run from Canada into northern California. Mount Hood, the highest peak in Oregon—11,245 feet above sea level—is in the Cascades.

The Klamath Mountains are in the southwestern corner of Oregon. Thick forests clothe the mountainsides and many game animals live here. Farms and sheep ranches are common in the area, which is also rich in mineral resources such as nickel.

The Columbia Plateau covers most of eastern Oregon and extends into Washington and Idaho. This is where Oregon's vast wheat fields are located. There are also mountains in the region, as well as huge forests and deep canyons. Much of the land has been made productive by irrigation.

Above:
Eastern Oregon has much of the state's flat, open land, on which cattle and wheat are raised.

At left:
Mount Hood, in the Cascade Mountains, is the state's highest peak. The Cascade Range extends from northern to southern Oregon, with many elevations of 10,000 feet or more.

The Basin and Range Region covers part of southeastern Oregon and extends into California and other nearby states. This is mainly a high basin with few mountains, but the Cascade Range to the west cuts off moisture-bearing winds from the ocean and turns this territory into a semi-desert, suitable mainly for sheep and cattle ranching.

Oregon has a coastline of 296 miles, and much of the shore is quite rugged. The most important rivers in Oregon are the Columbia, the Willamette, and the Snake. There are many great lakes in Oregon, especially in the Cascade Mountains. The most famous is Crater Lake, 1,932 feet deep, which is the deepest lake in the United States. It was formed in the basin of an extinct volcano.

Along the coast, Oregon's climate is mild and moist, due in part to warm ocean currents. Rainfall, most common in the fall and winter, is about 75 inches per year. Portland, some 100 miles from the coast, has average January temperatures of about 38 degrees Fahrenheit, and average summer temperatures of only 67 degrees F. In the eastern half of the state, beyond the Cascade Range, the climate is so dry that average rainfall amounts to only a little more than 10 inches per year, and summers are generally hot.

Below right:
The Basin and Range Region, in southeast Oregon, is generally rocky and dry. The Cascade Mountains to the west cut off moisture-bearing winds from the Pacific Ocean.

Below:
Many of Oregon's lakes are in the central region, where drainage from the Cascade and Blue Mountains provides an abundant water supply.

The Lewis and Clark expedition was one of the first to explore the Oregon Territory. They employed the services of an Indian woman, Sacagawea, to act as interpreter for the group.

The History

There were many Indian tribes living in the Oregon territory when the first Europeans arrived. The Chinook fished for salmon along the lower Columbia River. In the northwest lived the Clackama, the Multnomah, and the Tillamook. East of the Cascade Range were the Bannock, the Cayuse, the Paiute, the Umatilla, and a branch of the Nez Percé. Along what is now the boundary between Oregon and California lived the Klamath and the Modoc.

Though the coast of Oregon was sighted and mentioned by Spanish navigators who went from Mexico to the Philippines in the 16th century, no one took much interest in it for quite a few years.

Some historians think that the English sea captain Sir Francis Drake may have touched on the Oregon southern coast in 1579 while searching for a route from the Northern Pacific to the Atlantic. Another British explorer, James Cook, discovered and named Cape Foulweather, north of Yaquina Bay, in 1778.

But Oregon attracted little attention until an American named Robert Gray sailed into and named the Columbia River in 1792. Soon after that, Meriwether Lewis and William Clark made the region famous with their report of its wealth and wonders. While on their exploratory trip through the Louisiana Purchase in 1805, they pioneered the route that would become the Oregon Trail, and their explorations, along with Gray's, gave the United States a strong claim to the Oregon territory.

In the early 1800s the Oregon region extended from Alaska (claimed by Russia) to California (claimed by Spain). East and west, it stretched from the Pacific to the Rocky Mountains. The fur trader John Jacob Astor created an American presence in Oregon when he built his trading post at Astoria in 1811. But he was frightened into selling it to the British North West Company during the War of 1812. Both the British and the Russians maintained their claims to Oregon.

In 1834 the first permanent American settlement was established by Methodist missionaries in the Willamette Valley. But population grew slowly, chiefly by way of wagon trains that had plodded across the mountains and prairie lands. Settlers were intent on building homes in forest clearings and farming the rich valleys. Many came from New England and gave such names as Portland, Salem, Medford, Albany, and Newport to their communities. Others were from the Middle West. In 1843 the region was proved accessible when a great wagon train led by Dr. Elijah White followed the Oregon Trail that began in Missouri.

From then on, hundreds of American settlers began arriving, and the United States government was motivated to settle its boundary disputes with Great Britain (Russia had given up its claims). In 1846

Fur trader John Jacob Astor established the post of Astoria in 1811. During the War of 1812, it was seized by the British, but Astor's American Fur Company set up other outposts that dominated the trade. Astor helped create a significant American presence in Oregon, where four nations—Russia, Spain, Great Britain, and the United States—were pressing their claims to the region.

the two countries agreed on the present dividing line of the 49th parallel as the boundary between the United States and Canada.

The Indian wars in Oregon—which were largely the result of treaty violations and excessive military force on the part of the United States government—began with the massacre of missionary Marcus Whitman and 11 others near Walla Walla (now in Washington) in 1847. This was followed by the Cayuse War of 1847, the Rogue River Wars of the 1850s, the Modoc War of 1872–73, the Nez Percé War of 1877, and the Paiute and Bannock Uprisings of 1878. Not until 1890 were the Indian wars effectively ended throughout the West.

In 1848 Oregon had become a territory, with its capital at Oregon City. The capital was moved to Salem in 1850. In 1855 Congress carved the Washington Territory out of the Oregon Territory, and in 1859, Oregon joined the Union as the 33rd state. Later the railroads linked it to the East, and the rate of settlement increased—farms, forests, fish, and furs were the attractions.

After the Civil War, veterans from both sides began arriving in Oregon to seek new opportunities. The population of the state increased sixfold in a mere 30 years. Women were given the right to vote and hold office in 1912.

During World War I, an astonishing 44,000 Oregonians served in the armed forces. Oregon became a "war-boom" state during World War II. Factories were producing military equipment; Portland became a major port from which this equipment was shipped to troops in the Pacific Theater; cargo vessels and warships were built.

Today, Oregon is on the move. Increased irrigation has opened vast new areas of farmland. Hydroelectric plants on the Columbia and Willamette River systems provide power that encourages industrial growth. The tourist industry is booming as a result of Oregon's many natural attractions and opportunities for outdoor sports, camping, boating, and other recreational activities.

Education

The first school in Oregon was established by a Methodist missionary, Jason Lee, at French Prairie in 1834. A free public-school system was mandated by law in 1849. By the time that Oregon became a state in 1859, it had four institutions of higher education: Willamette University (1842), Linfield College (1849), Pacific University (1849), and Oregon College of Education (1856).

Famous People

Many famous people were born in the state of Oregon. Here are a few:

Danny Ainge b. 1959, Eugene. Basketball player

Wally Backman b. 1959, Hillsboro. Baseball player

Daniel Barbey 1889-1969, Portland. U.S. naval officer

Blanche Bates 1873-1941, Portland. Stage actress

James Beard 1903-85, Portland. Cookbook author

Beverly Cleary b. 1916, McMinnville. Children's book author

Dean Cromwell 1879-1962, Turner. Track-and-field coach

Homer Davenport 1867-1912, Silverton. Cartoonist

Margaret Osborne duPont b. 1918, Joseph. Tennis champion

Herbert Gaston 1881-1956, Halsey. Journalist and government official

Alfred C. Gilbert 1884-1961, Salem. Business leader and

Jane Powell began her show business career as a child, singing on the radio.

toy manufacturer

Neil Goldschmidt b. 1940, Eugene. Secretary of Transportation

Morris Graves b. 1910, Fox Valley. Artist

Mark Hatfield b. 1922, Dallas. Senate leader

Willis Hawley 1864-1941, near Monroe. Educator and congressman

Margaux Hemingway b. 1955, Portland. Film

actress: *Lipstick*

Howard Hesseman b. 1940, Lebanon. Television and film actor: *WKRP in Cincinnati, Head of the Class*

Larry Jansen b. 1920, Verboort. Baseball pitcher

Joseph 1840-1904, Wallowa Valley. Indian leader

Dave Kingman b. 1948, Pendleton. Baseball player

Kenneth Latourette 1884-1968, Oregon City. Theologian

Mickey Lolich b. 1940, Portland. Baseball pitcher

Ranald MacDonald 1824-94, Fort George. Adventurer

Larry Mahan b. 1957, White Pass. Champion rodeo performer

Edwin Markham 1852-1940, Oregon City. Poet

Ross McIntire 1889-1959, Salem. Physician

Douglas McKay 1893-1959, Portland. Secretary of the Interior

Dale Murphy b. 1956, Portland. Baseball player

Brent Musburger b. 1939,

Portland. Broadcaster

Richard Neuberger 1912-60, Portland. Senate leader and journalist

Bob Packwood b. 1932, Portland. Senate leader

Linus Pauling b. 1901, Portland. Two-time Nobel Prize-winning chemist

River Phoenix 1970-93, Madras. Film actor: *My Own Private Idaho; Stand by Me*

Jane Powell b. 1929, Portland. Film actress: *Seven Brides for Seven Brothers, Deep in My Heart*

Ahmad Rashad b. 1949, Portland. Football player and broadcaster

Johnnie Ray 1927-90, Rosebud. Pop singer

John Reed 1887-1920, Portland. Journalist and political radical

Harold Reynolds b. 1960, Eugene. Baseball player

Susan Ruttan b. 1950, Oregon City. Television actress: *L.A. Law*

Patricia Schroeder b. 1940, Portland. Congresswoman

Doc Severinsen b. 1927, Arlington. Bandleader and trumpeter

Paul Simon b. 1928, Eugene. Senate leader

Sally Struthers b. 1948, Portland. Television actress: *All in the Family*

Colleges and Universities

There are many colleges and universities in Oregon. Here are the more prominent, with their locations, dates of founding, and enrollments.

Concordia College, Portland, 1905, 1,066

Eastern Oregon State College, La Grande, 1929, 2,117

George Fox College, Newberg, 1891, 1,257

Lewis and Clark College, Portland, 1867, 1,767

Linfield College, McMinnville, 1849, 1,468

Marylhurst College for Lifelong Learning, Marylhurst, 1893, 1,048

Oregon Health Sciences University, Portland, 1974, 392

Oregon Institute of Technology, Klamath Falls, 1947, 2,757

Oregon State University, Corvallis, 1868, 11,430

Pacific University, Forest Grove, 1849, 959

Reed College, Portland, 1904, 1,210

Southern Oregon State College, Ashland, 1926, 4,103

University of Oregon, Eugene, 1872, 13,097

University of Portland, Portland, 1901, 2,254

Western Oregon State College, Monmouth, 1856, 3,647

Willamette University, Salem, 1842, 1,626

Where To Get More Information
Tourism Division
Oregon Dept of Economic Development
775 Summer St. NE
Salem, OR 97310
1-800-543-8838 (in Oregon)
1-800-547-7842 (outside Oregon)

Washington

On the seal of the state of Washington is a picture of George Washington, along with the date 1889—the year of the state's admission to the Union. "The Seal of the State of Washington" is printed in the outer circle.

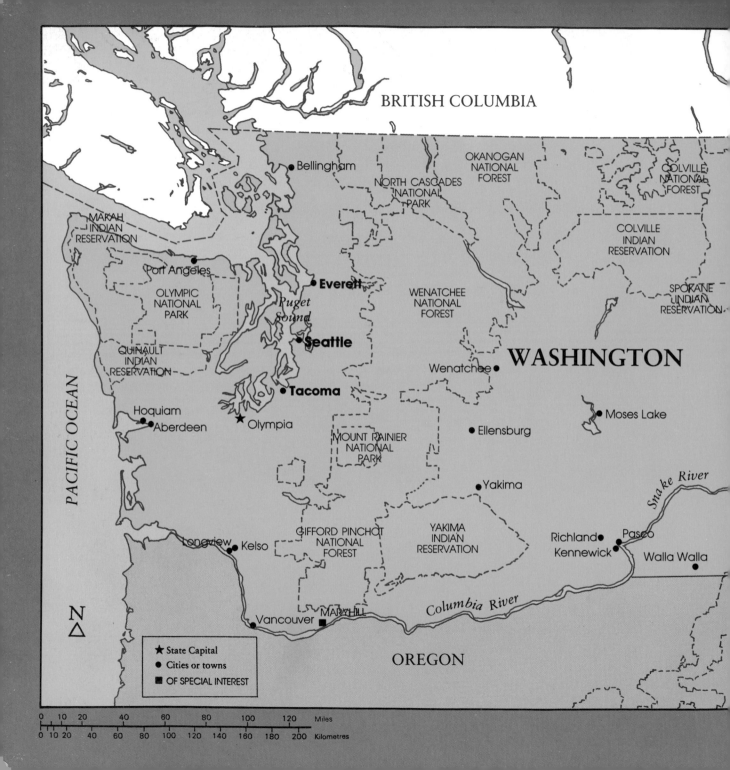

WASHINGTON
At a Glance

Capital: Olympia

State Flag

Major Crops: Grains, apples, potatoes, hay

Major Industries: Aerospace, forest products, refining, agriculture

IDAHO

Spokane
Opportunity
Pullman

Size: 68,139 square miles (20th largest)
Population: 5,135,731 (16th largest)

State Flower: Western Rhododendron
State Bird: Willow Goldfinch

73

State Flag

The state flag of Washington was adopted in 1923 and changed slightly in 1925. The dark green field, which sometimes is fringed, contains the state seal in the center.

State Motto

Alki

The state motto is a Chinook Indian word meaning "By and by." It appeared on the territorial seal designed by Lieutenant J. K. Duncan.

In 1788, Captain John Meares named this range the Olympic Mountains because he felt the peaks were fit to house the gods.

State Capital

Olympia became the territorial capital in 1855 and continued as the state capital after 1889.

State Name and Nickname

The state of Washington was named for George Washington, the first president of the United States.

The official nickname of the state is the *Evergreen State* because of its many large fir and pine trees. Another nickname, no longer used, is the *Chinook State*, referring to the salmon industry and to the Chinook Indians.

State Flower

The western rhododendron, *Rhododendron macrophyllum*, was designated state flower in 1949.

State Tree

In 1947, the western hemlock, *Tsuga heterophylla*, was selected as state tree.

State Bird

The willow goldfinch, *Astragalinus tristis salicamans*, was adopted as state bird in 1951.

State Dance

The square dance was chosen state dance in 1979.

State Fish

In 1969, the Steelhead trout, *Salmo gairdnerii*, was named state fish.

State Gem

Petrified wood was adopted as state gem in 1975.

State Song

"Washington My Home," words and music by Helen Davis, was chosen state song in 1959.

Population

The population of Washington in 1992 was 5,135,731, making it the 16th most populous state. There are 68.25 people per square mile.

Industries

The principal industries of the state are aerospace, forest products, food products, primary metals, tourism, and agriculture. In 1990 tourists spent $5.3 billion in Washington. The chief manufactured products are aluminum, and processed fruits and vegetables.

Agriculture

The chief crops of the state are hops, spearmint oil, raspberries, apples, asparagus, pears, cherries, peppermint oil, and potatoes. Washington is also a livestock state. There are estimated to be 1.3 million cattle, 50,000 hogs and pigs, 59,000 sheep, and 5.7 million chickens and turkeys on its farms. Douglas fir, hemlock, cedar, and pine are harvested. Construction sand and gravel, crushed stone, and Portland cement are important mineral products. Commercial fishing earned $104.5 million in 1992.

Government

The governor is elected for a

four-year term, as are the lieutenant governor, secretary of state, treasurer, auditor, attorney general, superintendent of public instruction, commissioner of public lands, and insurance commissioner. The state legislature, which meets annually, consists of a 49-member senate and a 98-member house of representatives. Each of the 49 legislative districts elects one senator and two representatives. Senators serve four-year terms, while representatives serve two-year terms. The present constitution, adopted in 1889, has been amended more than 60 times. In addition to its two United States senators, Washington has nine representatives in the U.S. House of Representatives. The state has eleven votes in the electoral college.

14,410-foot Mount Rainier was named by George Vancouver for his friend Peter Rainier.

Sports

Many sporting events on the collegiate and secondary school levels are played throughout the state. In football, the University of Washington won the Rose Bowl in 1960, 1961, 1978, 1982, and 1991, and the Orange Bowl in 1985. Washington State University was triumphant in the Rose Bowl in 1916. The University of Washington has also been strong in the sport of rowing, with its women's team winning the Collegiate Varsity Eights championship in 1981, 1982, 1983, 1984, 1985, 1987, and 1988, and the men's team winning in 1984. In baseball, the team from Kirkland won the Little League World Series in 1982.

On the professional level, the Seattle Mariners of the American League play baseball in the Kingdome, which they share with the Seattle Seahawks of the National Football League. The Seattle SuperSonics of the National Basketball

Association play their home games in the Coliseum.

Major Cities

Seattle (population 516,259). Founded in 1852 and named for a local Indian chief, Seattle is located on a narrow strip of land between Puget Sound and Lake Washington. About 2,000 ocean-going cargo ships visit this busy port each year. Much of its modern skyline owes its existence to the Century 21 Exposition of 1962. The "Man in Space" exhibit was one of the few profitable expositions at any World's Fair. The West Coast's largest fishing fleet sails from Seattle.

Things to see in Seattle: Blake Island Marine State Park, Burke Museum, Center for Wooden Boats, Coast Guard Museum Northwest, Discovery Park, Ellis Park, Evergreen Point Floating Bridge, Fire Station No. 5, Fishermen's Terminal, Frye Museum, Henry Art Gallery, Kingdome, Lake Washington Ship Canal and Hiram M. Chittenden Locks, Museum of Flight, Museum of History and Industry, Nordic Heritage Museum, Pier 59, Seattle Aquarium, Fun Forest Amusement Park, Pacific Science Center, Seattle Children's Museum, Space Needle, Smith Tower, University of Washington Arboretum, Volunteer Park, Seattle Art Museum, Waterfront Park, Wing Luke Asian Museum, and Woodland Park Zoological Gardens.

Spokane (population 177,165). Settled in 1871, the city began as a sawmill at Spokane Falls. The coming of the railroads, along with the Idaho gold rush, sparked the city's growth. Despite suffering a devastating fire in 1889, Spokane has developed into the largest railroad center west of Omaha. It is estimated that approximately one fourth of the nation's stand of soft timber is in this region. Idaho white pine, ponderosa pine, sugar pine, and associated species are the main wood types produced here. The 1974 World's Fair was held in Spokane with the theme, "Celebrating Tomorrow's Fresh, New Environment." Spokane, with its successful manufacturing and timber industries, has become the economic and cultural center of the region.

Things to see in Spokane: Cathedral of St. John, Cheney Cowles Memorial Museum, Crosby Library, John A. Finch Arboretum, Manito Park, Mount Spokane, Museum of Native American Cultures, Riverfront Park, Splashdown Waterslide Park, Spokane House Interpretive Center, and Walk in the Wild.

Tacoma (population 176,664). The third-largest city in the state, it is located 30 miles south of Seattle on the Puget Sound. It was settled in 1852 by immigrants and entrepreneurs attracted by the substantial lumber. A Swedish immigrant, Nicholas De Lin, constructed the first water-driven mill and opened a brewery, barrel factory, and a salmon-packing plant. Originally called Commencement Bay by

The Grand Coulee Dam was built during the Great Depression, under President Franklin D. Roosevelt's plan to provide much-needed jobs with public projects. The dam is now one of the world's largest hydroelectric engineering works.

General Morton McCarver in 1868, the name was later changed to Tacoma, the Indian word for Mount Rainier. It is a leading port and industrial and wholesale center. With the Olympic Mountains to the northwest and snow-capped Mount Rainier to the east, Tacoma is popular among outdoor enthusiasts and offers many recreational opportunities. Tacoma is a thriving port of over 4,000 acres. Its principal cargo includes wheat, flour, and lumber.

Things to see in Tacoma:
Washington State Historical Museum, Tacoma Art Museum, Tacoma Narrows Bridge, McChord Air Force Base, Camp Murray, and Fort Lewis.

Places to Visit

The National Park Service maintains 10 areas in the state of Washington: Olympic National Park, Mount Rainier National Park, North Cascades National Park, Fort Vancouver National Historic Site, Whitman Mission National Historic Site, Ross Lake National Recreation Area, Lake Chelan National Recreation Area, Coulee Dam National Recreation Area, San Juan Island National Historical Park, and Klondike Gold Rush National Historical Park. In addition, there are 86 state recreation areas.

Bellingham: Whatcom Museum of History and Art. Housed in the former city hall, this museum features logging industry memorabilia, and changing art exhibits.

Black Diamond: Black Diamond Historical Museum. This museum contains replicas of a western jail and a country doctor's office among its exhibits.

Cle Elum: Cle Elum Historical Telephone Museum. This museum displays old telephones, switchboards, and other equipment.

Coulee Dam: Grand Coulee Dam. One of the largest concrete structures in the world, the dam provides electric power for the region.

Eatonville: Northwest Trek. Visitors may ride a tram through the 600-acre wildlife preserve which contains moose, caribou, elk, and other animals in their natural surroundings.

Ferndale: Hovander Homestead. This restored 1903 homestead includes a barn, milkhouse, and children's farm zoo.

Hoquiam: Hoquiam's "Castle." This turreted 20-room mansion, the former home of lumber tycoon Robert Lytle, is furnished with many antiques.

Ilwaco: Lewis and Clark Interpretive Center. The center details the two-and-a-half-year, 8,000-mile journey of Meriwether Lewis and William Clark.

Neah Bay: Makah Cultural and Research Center. The museum contains over 55,000 artifacts of the Makah and Northwest Coast Indians, some dating back 2,000 years.

Olympia: State Capitol Museum. Originally the home of Olympia mayor Clarence Lord, the museum contains exhibits pertaining to the government of Washington.

Omak: St. Mary's Mission. Founded by Father Etienne de Rougé in 1886, the mission stands next to Paschal Sherman Indian School, the only Indian boarding school in Washington.

Puyallup: Ezra Meeker Mansion. Built in 1890, this 17-room Victorian mansion was the home of the town's first mayor.

Richland: Hanford Science Center. This museum focuses on energy through hands-on exhibits and computerized games.

Sequim: Olympic Game Farm. This 90-acre preserve is home to many of the animals that appear in wildlife films and television.

Tacoma: Point Defiance Park. The 700-acre park features Fort Nisqually, Never Never Land, Point Defiance Zoo and Aquarium, and the Natural Habitat Aviary.

Events

There are many events and organizations that schedule activities of various kinds in the state of Washington. Here are some of them.

Sports: Rodeo Days (Cheney), Ellensburg Rodeo (Ellensburg), Silver Lake Triathlon (Everett), Scottish Highland Games (Ferndale), Capital City Marathon and Relay (Olympia), Omak Stampede and Suicide Race (Omak), Goodwill Games (Seattle), horseracing at Longacres Race Course (Seattle), Loggerodeo (Sedro Woolley), Diamond Spur Rodeo (Spokane), Lilac Bloomsday Run (Spokane).

Arts and Crafts: National Western Art Show and Auction (Ellensburg), Living Museum (Ephrata), Ezra Meeker Community Festival (Puyallup), Sunfest (Richland), Pacific Northwest Arts and Crafts Fair (Seattle), Western Art Show and Auction (Spokane).

Music: Mountaineers' Forest Theater (Bremerton), Jazz Unlimited (Pasco), Pacific Northwest Ballet (Seattle), Seattle Symphony (Seattle), Opera House and Convention Center (Spokane), Spokane Symphony (Spokane), Tacoma Symphony Orchestra (Tacoma).

Entertainment: Asotin County Fair (Asotin), Apple Days (Cashmere), King County Fair (Enumclaw), Salty Sea Days (Everett), Washington State International Air Fair (Everett), Fall Foliage Festival (Federal Way), Old Settlers Pioneer Days Picnic (Ferndale), Ski to Sea

Festival (Ferndale), Yakima Valley Junior Fair (Grandview), Christmas Lighting Festival (Leavenworth), Maifest (Leavenworth), Washington State Autumn Leaf Festival (Leavenworth), Strawberry Festival (Marysville), Loggers Jubilee (Morton), Skagit Valley Tulip Festival (Mount Vernon), Makah Days (Neah Bay), Holland Happening (Oak Harbor), Capitol Lakefair (Olympia), Harbor Days (Olympia), Sunflower Festival (Omak), Rhododendron Festival (Port Townsend), Skandia Midsommarfest (Poulsbo), Vikingfest (Poulsbo), Yule Log Festival (Poulsbo), Daffodil Festival (Puyallup), Western Washington State Fair (Puyallup), Heritage Festival (Redmond), Bumbershoot (Seattle), Harvest Festival (Seattle), Northwest Folklife Festival (Seattle), Norwegian Constitution Day (Seattle), Seattle Seafair (Seattle), Irrigation Festival (Sequim), West Coast Oyster Shucking Contest (Shelton), Evergreen State Fair (Snohomish), Interstate Fair (Spokane), Lilac Festival (Spokane), Toppenish Creek Encampment (Toppenish), Apple Blossom Festival (Wenatchee), Lilac Festival (Woodland), Central Washington Fair (Yakima).

Two women participate in the log-rolling competition at the Loggers Jubilee.

Tours: Boeing 747-767 Division (Everett), Victorian Homes Tour (Port Townsend), Seattle Harbor Tour (Seattle), Annual Homes Tour (Snohomish), Tacoma Harbor Tour (Tacoma).

Theater: Laughing Horse Summer Theatre (Ellensburg), A Contemporary Theater (Seattle), Bagley Wright Theatre (Seattle), 5th Avenue Theatre (Seattle), The Indian Dinner Theatre (Seattle), Intiman at the Seattle Center Playhouse (Seattle), Omnidome Film Experience (Seattle), IMAX Theatre (Spokane), Spokane Civic Theatre (Spokane).

Nicknamed the *Evergreen State*, Washington is teeming with forests of fir and pine and overflowing with lakes and rivers, making lumbering and fishing important state industries. Most of the state's residents live along the many arms of Puget Sound. The cities in the region have grown in popularity recently for their prosperity, scenic beauty, and thriving cultural scene.

Apple blossoms flower in the hills of Washington, which leads the nation in commercial apple production. The state earns more than $290,000,000 annually through the sale of fruits, nuts, and berries.

The Land and the Climate

Washington is bounded on the west by the Pacific Ocean, on the north by the Canadian province of British Columbia, on the east by Idaho, and on the south by Oregon. The state has six main land areas: the Olympic Mountains, the Coast Range, the Puget Sound Lowland, the Cascade Mountains, the Columbia Plateau, and the Rocky Mountains.

The Olympic Mountains are located in the northwestern peninsula of Washington; most of the area is within Olympic National Park. Here are rugged, snow-covered mountains filled with wildlife and beautiful scenery and an unspoiled coastline still inhabited by its native Makah Indians. The main industry is logging in the mountains' foothills.

The Coast Range is in the southwestern corner of Washington. The most important industries here are logging and lumbering, but the fishing and dairy industries help support the region's economy.

The Puget Sound Lowland is located between the Olympic Mountains and the Coast Range, and extends east of these two regions to form a belt from the northern to the southern borders of the state. More than two-thirds of Washington's residents live here. It is a region of scenic and prosperous cities connected by the many arms of Puget Sound. Poultry and dairy farms and fruit orchards also flourish here.

The Cascade Mountains are east of the Puget Sound Lowland. These mountains, formed by volcanic activity, are part of a long chain that extends from British Columbia to northern California. In Washington the Cascades include Mount Rainier, the range's highest peak at 14,410 feet. In 1980 long-dormant Mount St. Helens erupted suddenly in a devastating display that spread destruction for a hundred miles around. This is a land of vast forests, mountain lakes, and glaciers. Copper, gold, and coal are mined here.

Mount St. Helens, in the Cascade Range, is one of the nation's few active volcanoes. Dormant for many years, it erupted unexpectedly in 1980, causing serious damage.

Below right:
The Columbia River, one of the state's major sources of water and hydroelectric power, forms much of Washington's southern border. Descending from Canada to flow west to the Pacific, the river is the most important in the Northwest.

Below:
The fertile soil of central and southeastern Washington is ideal for farming. In the southern coastal region, where the climate is suited to grape-growing, vineyards produce wines of excellent quality.

The Columbia Plateau covers most of central and southeastern Washington. It is a basin lying from 500 to 2,000 feet above sea level. The soil is extremely fertile, although this arid region receives little rainfall. Farmers here use irrigation to raise beef and dairy cattle, sugar beets, hops, potatoes, and fruit. The hilly Palouse country in the southeast produces most of the state's valuable wheat crop.

The steep Rocky Mountains extend through the northeast corner of Washington. This branch of the Rockies is called the Okanogan Range, and its major industry is mining—copper, gold, lead, magnesite, silver, and zinc.

Washington's coastline along the Pacific Ocean measures 157 miles, but its total shoreline is 3,026 miles, including the land along the Strait of Juan de Fuca in the northeast and vast Puget Sound with its numerous islands. The most important rivers in Washington include the Columbia, the Snake, the Colville, the Okanogan, the Chehalis, and the Cowlitz. There are many lakes in the state, some of them formed by ancient glaciation.

Western Washington, with its prevailing westerly winds and a coast washed by warm ocean currents, has a temperate marine climate, with cool summers and mild, somewhat rainy, winters. Seattle's average temperatures range from 64 degrees Fahrenheit in July to 38 degrees F. in January. On the Olympic Peninsula, just west of Seattle, the seaward slopes of the mountains have the heaviest rainfall in the United States—up to 140 inches a year. But eastern Washington has a dry, continental type of climate, with rainfall as low as 6 inches and no higher than 20 inches a year. Spokane, the chief city of eastern Washington, has an average July temperature of 74 degrees F. and an average January temperature of 25 degrees F.

Washington's total shoreline measures more than 3,000 miles, including the countless islands and coves of Puget Sound, an arm of the Pacific. The coast has many rocky cliffs and shoals that shipwrecked explorers and mariners, who named such sites as Cape Disappointment.

The History

This totem is an example of the expert woodcarving done by the coastal Indians of the Northwest and Canada, who hunted, gathered wild plants, and went to sea in large dugouts made from the region's tall trees.

Many Northwestern Indians were living in what is now Washington when European explorers arrived. East of the Cascades, in the plains and river valleys, were the Plateau Indians: the Cayuse, Colville, Nez Percé, Okinagan, Spokane, Yakima, and others. Along the coast were the Chinook, Clallam, Clatsop, Nisqually, Nooksak, and Puyallup. The coastal Indians were hunter-gatherers who depended upon fish, especially salmon, in addition to game animals. They were skilled woodcarvers, producing canoes and other utilitarian objects as well as ceremonial masks and totem poles. The Plateau Indians were hunters and gatherers who also fished in the region's streams and rivers.

In the 16th century, Spanish and English explorers skirted the coast of Washington, but the region was little known until some 200 years later. In the late 18th century, the Spaniards in California feared that the Russians in Alaska might lay claim to the Pacific Northwest, so they sent several expeditions to the territory. In 1775 Bruno Heceta and Juan Francisco de la Bodega y Quadra were the first to land in what would become Washington, near present-day Point Grenville, where they claimed the region for Spain. The British also believed that they had some title to the area after James Cook sailed along the coast and George Vancouver made a survey of Puget Sound and the Gulf of Georgia between 1792 and 1794. The United States based its claim on the explorations of Captain Robert Gray, who discovered the mouth of the Columbia River in 1792. In 1805 Meriwether Lewis and William Clark, who had been sent by President Thomas Jefferson to explore the upper Louisiana Territory and to seek a passage to the Pacific Ocean, arrived in the Columbia River country. They described southern Washington as part of the Oregon Country in the journal of their explorations, and three widely separated settlements were founded not long afterward. The

Fort Vancouver was established by Great Britain in 1825 on the Columbia River, near what is now Portland, Oregon. It was built by the Hudson's Bay Company, which had trading networks throughout the Northwest.

English established Fort Vancouver, on the Columbia, to help develop the fur trade for the Hudson's Bay Company. On the eastern side of the region, Walla Walla became a supply center for nearby gold strikes, and Presbyterian missionaries led by Marcus and Narcissa Whitman founded a mission there in 1836. Roman Catholic missionaries established a presence on Puget Sound in 1839.

Many Americans came to the Northwest in the 1840s, as the Oregon Trail opened the region to settlement. In 1846 Great Britain and the United States settled a long-standing border dispute by assigning land north of the 49th parallel to Canada and lands south of that point to the United States. The vast Oregon Territory was created in 1848 and subdivided into the Oregon and Washington Territories in 1853. At the time, the Washington Territory included not only the future state of Washington, but also northern Idaho and western Montana. In 1859 the territory was expanded to include parts of what are now southern Idaho and Wyoming. Washington's present eastern boundary was set when the Idaho Territory was established in 1863.

Mountain barriers and Indian wars deterred heavy settlement of Washington until railroad service to the East began in 1883. Over the next 10 years, the population of Washington quadrupled. Seattle became a major and increasingly cosmopolitan port—the gateway to Alaska, British Columbia, and the Far East. The Alaskan Gold Rush helped turn the city into a prosperous maritime crossroad. In 1889 Washington joined the Union as the 42nd state.

During the early 20th century, lumbering and fishing developed into important industries. Irrigation of arid eastern Washington made it possible to cultivate wheat and fruit on a large scale. Food-processing plants and canneries were built. During World War I, which the United States entered in 1917, shipbuilding became a major industry, based around Puget Sound. Aircraft construction came to the fore during World War II, and extensive dams on the Columbia River provided more electric power for industry and water for irrigation, drawing thousands of new residents to the central valley during the 1950s. The dams also fostered the development of interior ports and shipping by taming the turbulent waters of Washington's rivers.

Today, Washington is prospering through good management of its vast natural resources. It has addressed the task of diversifying its industries, many of which are highly dependent upon government contracts, especially in the aerospace field. The state attracts more visitors every year, especially since the 1962 Seattle World's Fair increased awareness of Washington's many recreational facilities. Tourism was a $3 billion business in the early 1980s. Metal products, pulp and paper, and processed foods all contribute to the state's economy.

Education

The first school in what is now Washington opened in 1832 at Old Fort Vancouver to teach the children of those employed by the Hudson's Bay Company. Missionaries were teaching Indian children near present-day Spokane and Walla Walla in the 1830s. The statewide system of public schools was established in 1895.

At left:
Seattle is the largest city in Washington and is the state's most important cultural center, with a wide variety of museums, theaters, and the nationally acclaimed Seattle Symphony Orchestra.

Below:
Bavarian dancers in traditional costume celebrate at one of Washington's international festivals. The state's many ethnic groups include Americans of Japanese, Chinese, and Philippine descent who crossed the Pacific from the Far East.

Washington's first institution of higher education was Whitman College, founded in 1859. By the time that Washington became a state in 1889, there were three more—the University of Washington (1861), Gonzaga University (1887), and the University of Puget Sound (1888). Before the end of the century, 10 more colleges and universities had been established in the state.

The People

Approximately 81 percent of Washingtonians live in metropolitan areas. About 93 percent of them were born in the United States, including many Americans of Asian descent. Of the foreign-born groups, the largest are the Canadians and the Scandinavians. The largest religious membership is held by the Roman Catholics, while the Methodists and Lutherans comprise the largest Protestant groups. Other major denominations are the Baptists, Disciples of Christ, Episcopalians, Mormons, and Presbyterians.

Famous People

Many famous people were born in the state of Washington. Here are a few:

Earl Anthony b. 1930, Kent. Champion bowler

Earl Averill 1902-83, Snohomish. Hall of Fame baseball player

Mildred Bailey 1907-51, Tekoa. Jazz singer

Howard Blakeslee 1880-1952, New Dungeness. Science writer and editor

Bobby Brown b. 1924, Seattle. Baseball player and American League president

Scott Buchanan 1895-1968, Sprague. Philosopher and educator

Dyan Cannon b. 1937, Tacoma. Film actress: *Bob and Carol and Ted and Alice*

Chester F. Carlson 1906-68, Seattle. Physicist and inventor of xerography

Joanne Carner b. 1939, Kirkland. Champion golfer

Horace Cayton 1903-70, Seattle. Sociologist and author

Ron Cey b. 1948, Tacoma. Baseball player

Carol Channing b. 1921, Seattle. Stage actress: *Gentlemen Prefer Blondes, Hello Dolly!*

Judy Collins b. 1939, Seattle. Folk singer

Bing Crosby 1904-77, Tacoma. Singer and Academy Award-winning film actor: *Going My Way, High Society*

Constance Cummings b. 1910, Seattle. Tony Award-winning actress: *Wings*

Merce Cunningham b. 1919, Centralia. Choreographer

Glen Edwards 1907-73, Mold. Football player

Daniel J. Evans b. 1925, Seattle. Governor of Washington

Muir Fairchild 1894-1950, Bellingham. Army and air force officer in World War I

Frederick Faust 1892-1944, Seattle. Novelist: *The Untamed, Destry Rides Again*

Spokane Garry 1811-92, Spokane County. Indian leader

Jimi Hendrix 1942-70, Seattle. Rock guitarist

Frank Herbert 1920-86, Tacoma. Novelist: *Dune, Dragon in the Sea*

Bob Houbregs b. 1932, Seattle. Hall of Fame basketball player

Fred Hutchinson 1919-64, Seattle. Baseball manager

Henry Jackson 1912-83, Everett. Senate leader

Robert Joffrey 1930-88, Seattle. Choreographer

Dudley Knox 1877-1960, Walla Walla. Naval officer and historian

Leschi ?-1858, near the Nisqually River. Indian leader

Karl Llewellyn 1893-1962, West Seattle. Legal philosopher and educator

Kenny Loggins b. 1948, Everett. Pop singer

Phil Mahre b. 1957, White Pass. Ski champion

Kevin McCarthy b. 1914, Seattle. Film actor: *Invasion of the Body Snatchers, A Gathering of Eagles*

Mary McCarthy 1912-89, Seattle. Novelist and critic: *The Group, Memories of a Catholic Girlhood*

Guthrie McClintic 1893-1961, Seattle. Theatrical producer and director

Robert Motherwell 1915-1991, Aberdeen. Artist

Patrice Munsel b. 1925, Spokane. Operatic singer

Randy Myers b. 1962, Vancouver. Baseball pitcher

Gene Nelson b. 1920, Seattle. Dancer and film actor: *The West Point Story, Oklahoma!*

Janis Paige b. 1922, Tacoma. Film and stage actress: *Please Don't Eat the Daisies, The Pajama Game*

Clyde Pangborn 1894-1958, Bridgeport. Aviator

Dixie Lee Ray 1914-94, Tacoma. Governor and head of U.S. Atomic Energy Commission

Jimmie Rodgers b. 1933, Camas. Pop singer

Ryne Sandberg b. 1959, Spokane. Baseball player

Ron Santo b. 1940, Seattle. Baseball player

John Stockton b. 1962, Spokane. Basketball player

Robert Stroud 1890-1963, Seattle. Ornithologist known as "The Bird Man of Alcatraz"

Genevieve Taggard 1894-1948, Waitsburg. Poet: *Travelling Standing Still*

Audrey-May Wurdemann 1911-60, Seattle. Pulitzer Prize-winning poet: *Bright Ambush*

Colleges and Universities

There are many colleges and universities in Washington. Here are the more prominent, with their locations, dates of founding, and enrollments.

Central Washington University, Ellensburg, 1891, 7,016
Eastern Washington University, Cheney, 1890, 7,041
Evergreen State College, Olympia, 1967, 3,136
Gonzaga University, Spokane, 1887, 2,932
Pacific Lutheran University, Tacoma, 1890, 2,964
Seattle Pacific University, Seattle, 1891, 2,218
Seattle University, Seattle, 1892, 3,193
University of Puget Sound, Tacoma, 1888, 2,824
University of Washington, Seattle, 1861, 25,482
Walla Walla College, College Place, 1892, 1,639
Washington State University, Pullman, 1890, 14,890
Western Washington University, Bellingham, 1893, 9,274
Whitman College, Walla Walla, 1859, 1,198
Whitworth College, Spokane, 1890, 1,410

Where To Get More Information

Travel Development Division
Dept. of Commerce and Economic Development
General Administration Bldg.
Olympia, WA 98504
or call, 1-800-544-1800

Further Reading

General

Grabowski, John F., and Patricia A. Grabowski. *State Reports: The Northwest.* New York: Chelsea House, 1992.

Alaska

Alaska: High Roads to Adventure. DC: National Geographic Society, 1976.

Carpenter, Allan. *Alaska*, rev. ed. Chicago: Childrens Press, 1979.

Heinrichs, Ann. *America the Beautiful: Alaska.* Chicago: Childrens Press, 1991.

Hunt, William R. *Alaska: A Bicentennial History.* New York: Norton, 1976.

Wheeler, Keith. *The Alaskans.* New York: Time, Inc., 1977.

Idaho

Carpenter, Allan. *Idaho*, rev. ed. Chicago: Childrens Press, 1979.

Fradin, Dennis B. *Idaho in Words and Pictures.* Chicago:

Childrens Press, 1980.

Jensen, Dwight W. *Discovering Idaho: A History.* Caldwell, ID: Caxton, 1977.

Kent, Zachary. *America the Beautiful: Idaho.* Chicago: Childrens Press, 1990.

Peterson, Frank Ross. *Idaho: A Bicentennial History.* New York: Norton, 1976.

Wells, Merle W., and Arthur A. Hart. *Idaho, Gem of the Mountains.* Northridge, CA: Windsor Publications, 1985.

Young, Virgil M. *The Story of Idaho.* Moscow: University Press of Idaho, 1977.

Oregon

Clark, Malcolm, Jr. *Eden Seekers: The Settlement of Oregon, 1818-1862.* Boston: Houghton Mifflin, 1981.

Dodds, Gordon B. *Oregon: A Bicentennial History.* New York: Norton, 1977.

Fradin, Dennis B. *Oregon in Words and Pictures.* Chicago:

Childrens Press, 1980.

Stein, R. Conrad. *America the Beautiful: Oregon.* Chicago: Childrens Press, 1989.

Thollander, Earl. *Back Roads of Oregon.* New York: Crown, 1979.

Washington

Atkeson, Ray A. *A Portrait of Washington.* Portland, OR: Graphic Arts Center, 1980.

Avery, Mary W. *Washington: A History of the Evergreen State*, rev. ed. Seattle: University of Washington Press, 1965.

Clark, Norman H. *Washington: A Bicentennial History.* New York: Norton, 1976.

Fradin, Dennis B. *Washington in Words and Pictures.* Chicago: Childrens Press, 1980.

Stein, R. Conrad. *America the Beautiful: Washington.* Chicago: Childrens Press, 1992.

Numbers in italics refer to illustrations

A

Agriculture (AK), 11, 18-19, 25; (ID), 35, 38, 39, 46; (OR), 55, 62, 64, 68; (WA), 73, 76, 84, 85, 86, 90
Alaska, 5-28; area, 7; capital, *7*, 10; climate, 20; government, 11; map, 6-7; places to visit, 13-15; population, 7, 10, 27; state bird, *7*, 10; state fish, 10; state flag, 9, *9*; state flower, *7*, 10; state gem, 10; state marine mammal, 10; state mineral, 10; state motto, 9; state name, 10; state seal, 5, *5*; state sport, 10; state song, 10; state tree, 10; as territory, 23-25
Alaskan pipeline, *19*, 25
Alaska Purchase, 23
Aleutian Islands, 18, 20, 21, 25
Aleuts, 21, 23, 27
American exploration/settlement (AK), 23-25; (ID), 42, 44, 45; (OR), *65*, 66-68; (WA), 88-90
Anchorage (AK), 12, *13*, 20
Arco (ID), 36, 46
Astor, John Jacob, 66, *67*
Athapaskan Indians, 21, 27

B

Bannock Indians, 35, 42, 45, 65, 67
Baranof, Alexander, 22, 23, 24
Barnette, Captain E.T., 12
Bering, Vitus, 21
Bering Strait, 21
Boise (ID), 34, 35, 45
British exploration/settlement (AK), 22; (OR), 66-67; (WA), 88-89

C

Canadian exploration/settlement, 42
Cascade Mountains, 62, *63*, 64, 65, 84, 85, *85*
Cayuse Indians, 65, 67, 88
Chief Joseph, *44*, 45
Chinook Indians, 65, 75, 88
Civil War, 68
Clackama Indians, 65
Clark, William, 42, *65*, 66, 88
Coeur d'Alene Indians, 42
Colleges and universities (AK), 28; (ID), 48; (OR), 70; (WA), 93

Columbia River, 39, 42, 64, 65, 66, 68, *86*, 87, 88, 90
Conestoga (covered) wagon, *42*, 66
Cook, James, *22*, 66, 88
Crater Lake (OR), *52-53*, 64

E

Education (AK), 26-27; (ID), 47; (OR), 68; (WA), 90-91
Eskimos (Inuit), 21, 22-23, 27
Events: arts and crafts (AK), 15; (ID), 37; (OR), 59; (WA), 80; entertainment (AK), 15; (ID), 37; (OR), 59; (WA), 80-81; music (AK), 15; (ID), 37; (OR), 59; (WA), 80; sports (AK), 11-12, 15; (ID), 35, 36-37; (OR), 55-56, 58-59; (WA), 77-78, 80; theater (AK), 15; (ID), 37; (OR), 59; (WA), 81; tourism information (AK), 28; (ID), 48; (OR), 70; (WA), 93; tours (AK), 15; (ID), 37; (OR), 59; (WA), 81
Exxon *Valdez*, 25

F

Fairbanks (AK), 12-13, 24
Famous people (AK), 28; (ID), 48; (OR), 69-70; (WA), 92-93

G

Gold rush, 12, 13, 23-24, 35, 45, 56, 78, 89-90
Gray, Robert, 66, 88
Great Depression, 46

H

Haida Indians, 21, 27
Hudson's Bay Company, 22, 89, 90

I

Idaho, 29-48; area, 31; capital, *31*, 34; climate, 39; government, 35; map, 30; places to visit, 36; population, 31, 34, 47; state bird, *31*, 34; state flag, 33, *33*; state flower, *31*, 34; state gem, 34; state horse, 34; state motto, 33; state name, 34; state seal, 29, *29*; state song, 34; state tree, 34; as territory, 45, 89
Industries (AK), 7, 10-11, 18-19; (ID), 31, 34,

38, 39, 46; (OR), 51, 55, 62, 68; (WA), 73, 76, 84, 85, 86, 90
Inuit. *See* Eskimos

J

Johnson, Andrew, 23
Juneau (AK), 10, 13, 14, *20*, 23, 24

K

Klamath Indians, 65
Klondike, the. *See* Yukon, Canadian
Kutenai Indians, 42

L

Lapwai Reservation (ID), 44, 45
Lewis, Meriwether, 42, 66, 88
Lewiston (ID), 34, 36, 42, 45

M

Modoc Indians, 65, 67
Monroe Doctrine, 23
Mormons, 42, 45
Mount Hood (OR), 62, *63*
Mount McKinley (AK), 18
Mount Rainier (WA), *77*, 79
Mount St. Helens (WA), 85, *85*
Multnomah Indians, 65

N

Nez Percé Indians, 42, *44*, 45, 65, 88
Nez Percé War, 44, 45, 67, 87
Northwest Coast Indians, 21, 23, *26*, 27, *88*

O

Olympia (WA), 76
Olympic Mountains, *74-75*, 79, 84
Oregon, 49-70; area, 51; capital, *51*, 54; climate, 64; government, 55; map, 50-51; places to visit, 57-58; population, 51, 54-55; state animal, 54; state bird, *51*, 54; state dance, 54; state fish, 54; state flag, 53, *53*; state flower, *51*, 54; state gemstone, 54; state insect, 54; state motto, 53; state name, 54; state rock, 54; state seal, 49, *49*; state song, 54; state tree, 54; as territory, 68, 89
Oregon Trail, 42, 66, 89

P

Paiute Indians, 65, 67
Pend d'Oreille Indians, 42
Peter the Great, czar of Russia, 21
Pocatello (ID), 35-36
Portland (OR), 56-57, 66, 68
Pound, Ezra, 47, 48
Powell, Jane, 69, 70
Puget Sound, 78, 85, 87, 89, 90
Puyallup Indians, 88

R

Rocky Mountains, 18, 19, 38, 84, 86
Russian-American Company, 22-23, 24
Russian claims, Northwest, 21-22, 23, 66, 88
Russian exploration/settlement, 21-22, 23

S

Sacagawea, 48, 65

Salem (OR), 54, 56, 66, 68
Seattle (WA), 78, 87, 89-90, 91
Seward, William H., 23, 23
Shoshone Indians, 42, 43
Siberia, 19, 21, 22, 23
Sitka (AL), 15, 22, 23, 24, 24
Snake River, 38, 39, 64, 87
Spalding, Henry H., 42, 47
Spanish claims, Northwest, 66, 67, 88
Spokane (WA), 78, 87, 90
Spokane Indians, 88

T

Tacoma (WA), 78-79
Tillamook Indians, 65
Tlingit Indians, 14, 21, 23, 26, 27
Tsimshian Indians, 65

U

Umatilla Indians, 65

W

War of 1812, 66, 67
Washington, 71-93; area, 73; capital, 73, 76; climate, 87; government, 76-77; map, 72; places to visit, 79-80; population, 73, 76, 91; state bird, 76; state dance, 76; state fish, 76; state flag, 75, 75; state flower, 76; state gem, 76; state motto, 75; state name, 76; state seal, 71, 71; state song, 76; state tree, 76; as territory, 89-90
White Bird Canyon, battle of, 44, 45
World War I, 46, 68, 90
World War II, 12, 13, 24-25, 46, 68, 90

Y

Yukon, Canadian, 23-24

Picture Credits

Courtesy of Alaska Division of Tourism: pp. 3 (top), 5, 7, 8-9, 10, 11, 12, 13, 14, 16-17, 18, 19, 20, 24, 26; Courtesy of Dolly Wares Doll Museum: p. 58; Courtesy of Michael Guryan: p. 37; Courtesy of Idaho Secretary of State: p. 29; Courtesy of Idaho Travel Council: pp. 3 (bottom), 31, 38, 39, 40-41, 42, 46, 47 (top); Library of Congress: p. 22; Courtesy of Movie Material Store: p. 69; Museum of the American Indian: pp. 27, 43; Courtesy of National Park Service: pp. 52-53; Courtesy of National Park Service/Stoughton: p. 34; Courtesy of National Park Service/Woodbridge Williams: pp. 32-33; National Portrait Gallery/Smithsonian Institution: pp. 23, 44, 47 (bottom), 67; Courtesy of Oregon Tourism Division: pp. 4 (top), 49, 51, 57, 59, 60-61, 62, 63, 64; Courtesy of Portland Trail Blazers/Brian Drake: p. 56; The Smithsonian Collection: p. 65; Courtesy of State of Washington Tourism Division: pp. 4 (bottom), 73, 74-75, 77, 79, 81, 82-83, 84, 85, 86, 87, 88, 89, 91; Courtesy of Washington Secretary of State: p. 71.
Cover photos courtesy of Alaska Division of Tourism; Nevada Commission on Tourism; Oregon Tourism Division; and State of Washington Tourism Division.